"Comprehensive research and strategic future real estate success. The Swanepoel Trends Report represents the gold standard for third party independent scholarship pertaining to this all-important process."

Gino Blefari, *CEO, HSF Affiliates*

"The Swanepoel Trends Report is one of the most important and influential analyses available in real estate. I always enjoy reading it, and it helps shape the future of our industry. Thanks to Stefan and the entire team at T3 Sixty for the hard work that goes into this report. Our industry is grateful for it."

Spencer Rascoff, CEO, Zillow Group

"In my position, I need to always be looking around corners to see what's coming next. The Swanepoel Trends Report is like having a mirror on the end of a 10-foot pole."

Geoff Lewis, President, Re/Max

"The information provided in the Swanepoel Trends Report is invaluable to our industry. Stefan's presentation of factual analysis related to events, ideas, and technology, which inform the direction of our businesses, is second to none. I keep it on my desk all year long and encourage everyone who wishes to remain relevant tomorrow to absorb the information today."

Sue Yannaccone, President & CEO, ERA Franchise Systems

"We greatly value the Swanepoel Trends Report. I have always felt Stefan's work is critically important to our industry because of his unique insights and desire to go beyond the metrics we all routinely look at. While there is quite a lot of industry discussion about disruptors, impact of technology and the emergence of millennials, it challenges us to think differently and offers unique ideas, suggestions and potential solutions."

Charlie Young, President & CEO, Coldwell Banker Real Estate

"To hell with CNN, we should all turn to you for updates."

Scott Stulich, Broker, Home Selling Assistance Platinum, Maryland

"The Swanepoel Trends Report is 'the' go-to book on what is happening within the industry, a great source of real information to help brokers and brands plan for what lies ahead. I have been a subscriber since inception. It gets better and better every year."

Sherry Chris, President & CEO, Better Homes and Gardens Real Estate

"We are successful because of the decisions we make each day. The Swanepoel Trends Report isn't just about the future — it's about what is happening now. It's reflective of those decisions being made now. Stefan challenges us to use this invaluable information to give us the ability to make it happen NOW. It is mandatory reading for our senior leadership. Stefan's research helps us all think about what needs to happen now and in the future."

Helen Hanna Casey, President, Howard Hanna Real Estate Services

"The Swanepoel Trends Report and the T3 Summit always deliver. They provide important and insightful analysis about the trends, people and companies in the real estate business."

Ryan O'Hara, CEO, Move, Inc.

"The Swanepoel Trends Report is always one of my 'go to' reference guides regarding future trends in the real estate vertical. Truly a phenomenal resource and one that provides great insight and value."

Bob Goldberg, CEO, National Association of Realtors

"The Swanepoel Trends Report is the industry's premier report regarding the key factors shaping the real estate business. It serves as a mirror to ensure that we continue to be a highly successful real estate company."

Lennox Scott, CEO, John L. Scott Real Estate

"The market to come is anybody's guess. However, your estimate and forecast hold the highest chance of being correct."

Paul J. Wells, Broker & Owner, Re/Max Northern Illinois

"Stefan's thoughtful, comprehensive and often eye-opening insights add tremendous value to our strategic thinking and business decision-making."

Pam O'Connor, President & CEO, Leading Real Estate Companies of the World

"The Swanepoel Trends Report sets a new standard for research on industry trends. I keep a copy on my desk, which I utilize often and share with my leadership, members and staff."

Bob Hale, CEO, Houston Association of Realtors

2018 Swanepoel Trends Report

13th Annual Edition

T3 Sixty   Research, Analysis, Solutions

Swanepoel Trends Report

Bronze medalist for best business reference, AXIOM Business Book Awards

Editorial Team

Editor-in-Chief
Stefan Swanepoel

Executive Editor
Paul Hagey

Managing Editor
Aman Daro

Contributing Editor
Jeremy Conaway

Technology Editor
Jack Miller

Staff Writers
Michele Conn, Jack Miller, Kevin McQueen, Thomas Mitchell and Tinus Swanepoel

Contributors
Russ Cofano, Rob Hahn and Amber Taufen

Design
Faire Projects

Editorial Assistant
Karen Smith

Published by RealSure, Inc and T3 Sixty, LLC
29222 Rancho Viejo Rd, Suite 221
San Juan Capistrano, CA 92675
949.627.8877

t360.com

ISBN 978-0-9777-634-9-8
Price $179.95 USA
Printed in the United States of America

Copyright © 2018 by RealSure, Inc.
All rights reserved.

Except as permitted under the United States Copyright Act of 1976, no part of this publication may be reproduced or distributed in any form or by any means or stored in a database or retrieval system without the prior written permission of the publisher. Images may be protected by copyright and should not be used without approval.

Most of the companies mentioned in this report own numerous trademarks and other marks. This report, the publishers, the author, the contributors or any other party involved in this Report in any way, will not seek to challenge or dilute any of these marks. Specifically, Realtor is a registered trademark of the National Association of Realtors.

Limit of Liability / Disclaimer of Warranty:

While the publisher, authors, contributors and editors have used their best efforts to present neutral, accurate, and reasonable views of the industry and its participants, they make no representation or warranties with respect to the accuracy or completeness of the contents of each publication and specifically disclaim any implied warranties.

T3 Sixty serves many companies and organizations stated in this report as a management consulting firm and may also, from time to time, be an investor in some of the companies mentioned in this report. However, no confidential information or information covered by a nondisclosure agreement was used.

References to companies, products and services also do not constitute or imply endorsement, and neither is any reference or absence of reference intended to harm, advantage or disadvantage a company or person. The publishers, editorial team and T3 Sixty shall not be liable for any loss or any other commercial damages, including but not limited to special, incidental, consequential or other damages.

Table of Contents

viii **Foreword**
by Glenn Kelman

xi **Preface**
by Stefan Swanepoel

12 **Trend 10**
Tightening of the Digital Grip

32 **Trend 09**
The Complex World of Commercial Real Estate

54 **Trend 08**
Smart CRMs Go Mainstream

70 **Trend 07**
The Big Four of Digital Real Estate

94 **Trend 06**
Design as a Service

112 **Trend 05**
Brokerage M&A Momentum Broadens

128 **Trend 04**
The Management-Empowered Brokerage Business Model

148 **Trend 03**
Rise of the Modern Discount Brokerage

170 **Trend 02**
Enter the Direct Buyer

186 **Trend 01**
Follow the Money

Foreword

The Fortress and the Ecosystem

It was a strange request.

Out of the blue, a competing broker invited me to lunch. He was on one side of the lake that divides Seattle, and I was on the other, so he and his partner offered to meet on an island in the middle. Driving over the bridge, it bothered me that I was apprehensive. Why should I feel that way?

When I sat down, the broker spread his firm's training materials before me. He wasn't arguing that his agents were better than Redfin's. He only wanted me to know that, for all of Redfin's claims about prioritizing customers over commissions, his agents were also trained to put customers first. I looked through his materials, which I would have been proud to use to train Redfin's agents. My face turned pink. I said I was sorry for claiming that Redfin's agents had different motivations than the agents at his firm. And, though we pay our agents differently, I've never made such claims again.

What was most remarkable was what happened next: He accepted the apology. He gave me a chance to change and, over time, to belong to this industry. It's rare for anyone, a spouse or a friend let alone a rival, to be willing to look at another person in a different light.

That was a decade ago. I still think about that lunch when reading bedtime books to my boys, who often interrupt to ask about each character: "Is he bad or good?" Whatever the moral is supposed to be, the story also trains us from the earliest age to sort people into heroes and villains. The "I" in the story is always the hero. This is why my then 7-year-old began to recognize one of his harmless classmates as Harry Potter's nemesis, Draco Malfoy. It's why partisan differences prevent Congress from passing commonsense laws. It's why the Packers hate the Vikings. And it's why the real estate industry has sometimes had a siege mentality, with members of the old guard warily eyeing the barbarians at the gate.

And it's why the Swanepoel Trends Report is so valuable. This report isn't a one-sided defense of traditional real estate, technology, real estate's practitioners or our critics. It's written with the savvy of an insider and the curiosity of an outsider, so that we can see the forces now affecting our industry that have been hidden in plain sight. It gives us a chance to change, because seeing someone else in a new light is the only way we can also see ourselves in a new light.

The Changes Ahead

There's plenty to learn about in 2018. The expansionary fiscal policy of the last decade has generated nearly free capital, which has not only funded a runup in real estate prices but also in real estate technology. In 2013, $451 million was invested in real estate technology startups. It's projected to be $3 billion in 2017. This is an increase of $300 million from last year, but the number of firms who are getting that money dropped from 277 in 2016 to 61 this year.

The result: a new generation of well-funded potential disruptors is emerging, of Opendoors, OfferPads and Compasses. None so far as I know is vying to build another online portal. No company in a decade has tried to do that. Instead, each has a new way to sell houses, and each is chronicled here, with an explanation of how their business works.

An Ecosystem, Not a Fortress

But what I think is most valuable about this report is that it can be like the lunch I once had on an island in a lake with someone I thought I knew, but didn't know at all. This report can make us see the old divisions between websites and brokers, technologists and agents, in a new light.

The fortress the real estate industry has built to protect our data has turned us all into prisoners, squinting through arrow slits at a world we have forgotten is ours. Rather than trying to lock away our data we are, for the first time in a decade, in the process of ensuring we get credit for it, so that the customers who see our listings everywhere also see us, the agent and the broker, as the authoritative source of information about our local real estate market.

Seizing the future for ourselves is the whole premise of the Swanepoel Trends Report. It analyzes our industry as an ecosystem, rather than a fortress, in which every member contributes to the ecosystem, and each benefit as well. Virtually all our customers use a real estate website, but virtually every photo of every home on these sites was captured by a real estate agent, and conveyed to a database by that agent's brokerage. Every real estate site is thus the product of a collaboration with a million agents.

In this way, agents and brokers are the industry's eyes and ears, and also our hands and feet, working hard each day to host tours, negotiate sales, and prepare homes for sale. Above all, we're the industry's heart and soul, caring for people who have lost their jobs, their parents or their spouses, who have put everything they own into a U-Haul and begun the drive across the country toward a new life.

And of course, we as the agents and the brokers are the brains: No matter how much we may grumble about our own rules, we're still the ones who set and enforce them. Technology is the nervous system, connecting customers, agents and listings. As such, technology should benefit the whole ecosystem: the customers, the agents and the brokerages, not just the developers of that technology.

If this hasn't always been how the industry has worked out, we can change it. This after all is our industry, and we can make it what we want it to be. We can reimagine the relationships between agents, brokers and technology to benefit everyone.

That reimagining starts at least in part here, with a report that surveys everything that's changing in real estate, and a new way of seeing opportunities as threats, and rivals as partners and maybe even, to use one of Stefan's favorite words, as friends. So I hope this report shows us all new ways to work with one another, before we get back to the age-old business of beating each other's brains out over a listing consultation!

Glenn Kelman
CEO, Redfin
November 2017

T3 Sixty Publications
As of January 2018

2018	Swanepoel Trends Report
	Swanepoel Power 200
2017	MLS 2020 Agenda
	Commercial Real Estate ALERT
	Finding New Clarity
	Winning on the Web
	Swanepoel Trends Report
	Swanepoel Power 200
2016	Homeowner Insights
	Digitization of the Home Buying Process
	DANGER Report Canada
	Swanepoel Trends Report
	Swanepoel Power 200
2015	T3 Risk Guide
	DANGER Report USA
	T3 Tech Guide
	Swanepoel Trends Report
	Swanepoel Power 200
2014	Real Estate Confronts Agent Reviews
	Swanepoel Trends Report
	Swanepoel Power 200
2013	Swanepoel Technology Report
	Swanepoel Trends Report
2012	Swanepoel Trends Report
2011	Swanepoel Trends Report
2010	Swanepoel Trends Report
	Swanepoel Social Media Report
1997–2009	Swanepoel Trends Report (2009)
	Swanepoel Trends Report (2008)
	Swanepoel Trends Report (2007)
	Swanepoel Trends Report (2006)
	Real Estate Confronts Goal Setting vs. Business Planning (2005)
	Real Estate Confronts Bundled Services (2005)
	Real Estate Confronts Customer Acquisition (2004)
	Real Estate Confronts the Future (2004)
	Real Estate Confronts Profitability (2003)
	Real Estate Confronts the Banks (2002)
	Real Estate Confronts the e-Consumer (2000)
	Real Estate Confronts Technology (1999)
	Real Estate Confronts Reality (1997)

Preface

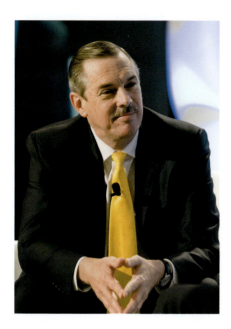

Change does not move in a straight line.

The past does not point directly toward the future. But with extensive research and thorough analysis, it is possible toward identify the biggest changes the industry will most likely face in the years to come. This is exactly what the Swanepoel Trends Report has done for 13 years.

As we look toward 2018 and beyond, we can see that the real estate industry is maturing. Multibillion dollar brokers are acquiring an increasing number of smaller organizations, and are changing the landscape in their wake. Professional investor financing is becoming a game-changer. Technology is changing buyer and seller expectations. Outside forces outside are affecting the way we do business.

Brokerages that are not learning from these trends may face a hard and startling future.

Optimistic brokers may look at their profit and growth and believe all is fine — they have little drive to evolve. But that is irresponsible and reckless. The industry is shifting under their feet, and streamlined, professionalized brokerage operations have never been as important as they are now. This is not fear-mongering or sensationalism, but an acceptance that change to our way of life is not just on the horizon — it is happening right now.

Real estate is your world — it is our world. We live it, breathe it, care for it, and analyze it. Our goal is to make this the best real estate report you will read this year. If you are holding it in your hands, set aside four hours and enjoy the most comprehensive strategic ride you can take, all the way back to the future of our industry.

Stefan Swanepoel
New York Times and Wall Street Journal Best-Selling Author,
Editor-in-Chief of the Swanepoel Trends Report
Chairman and CEO, T3 Sixty
December 2017

10 Tightening of the Digital Grip

Real Estate in the Year 2022

Technology has undeniably transformed the residential real estate industry. A glance through this report's table of contents makes it abundantly clear much more change is underway. Therefore, we decided to reach out to seven leaders at tech companies pushing the industry's envelope to get their visions for the industry's future. We do not necessarily support their views, but by getting a taste of their thinking and visions, we can all get a sense for the shape of things to come.

Technology Leaders' Vision of The Industry's Future

Eric Wu, Opendoor CEO and Co-Founder

Eric Wu has been CEO of Opendoor (opendoor.com) since co-founding it in 2014. Previously, he was founder and CEO of the geo-data analytics company Movity.com, which Trulia acquired in 2011. Wu led location, social and consumer product development at Trulia (trulia.com). He also co-founded RentAdvisor.com, which Apartment List acquired in 2013.

About Opendoor

With over $300 million in equity funding and more than 9,000 transactions under its belt, Opendoor is pioneering a new way for consumers to buy and sell homes. It marries brokerage operations with finance in a model the industry has come to know as iBuyers or Direct Buyers (see T3 Sixty's analysis of the Direct Buyer in Trend No. 2, "Enter the Direct Buyer.") Prominent Silicon Valley venture capitalist and former Square chief operating officer Keith Rabois, along with a team of seasoned real estate technology execs, founded the firm in 2014. Their goals are to add certainty, simplicity and shorter timelines to the homebuying process.

Like other Direct Buyer platforms such as OfferPad (offerpad.com), Opendoor is a brokerage as well as a homebuyer and seller. It purchases homes, charging sellers a convenience fee that ranges from 6 to 12 percent of the offer price (averaged 6.7 percent in September 2017), and prepares them to sell.

Sellers receive an offer from Opendoor often within 24 hours of requesting one; the offer remains valid for five days. When a seller accepts an offer, Opendoor can close on it in anywhere from three to 60 days with the timeline at the seller's discretion. The company also offers sellers lease-back options to add flexibility to the homeselling process.

Buyers can use Opendoor's app to access its listings and tour on their schedules from 6 a.m. to 9 p.m. seven days a week. They can also use the app to instantly make offers on an Opendoor home.

Opendoor Overview

Timeline	Founded and raised $10.0 million in mid-2014, raised an additional $20 million in February 2015, formally launched in June 2015 in Phoenix, raised $80 million in October 2015, raised $210 million in December 2016, launched mortgage and title divisions in September 2017.
Product/ Service	Simplifies homeselling by giving sellers fast offers, flexible, fast closing dates and certainty for a service fee. Allows buyers to tour homes and write offers at their convenience.
Growth	Nearly doubled employee count in 2017 with over 415 employees.
Scope/Scale	Opendoor operates in the metros of Phoenix; Dallas-Fort Worth; Las Vegas; Atlanta; Orlando, Florida and Raleigh, North Carolina.

Q: How do you think Opendoor will significantly or fundamentally change homebuying or the real estate industry?
A: Opendoor's mission is to empower everyone with the freedom to move. We have pioneered a revolutionary new way to move by shifting the home transaction online. By making buying and selling homes remarkably simple, we have removed the uncertainty, time and hassle from the home sale process. We believe consumers crave this today and will demand it in the future.

By dramatically simplifying how consumers sell and buy homes, we believe we can increase the frequency with which people move and the number of people who become homeowners. Whether our customers are moving for a job, sizing up for a new family, or downsizing for retirement, we want to make moving as easy as just making a few clicks.

Which technology or company, other than Opendoor, will also significantly change the real estate industry within five years?
Home Augmented Reality (Home AR). Homebuyers want to know a home they are evaluating can meet their specific needs. Home AR will enable home shoppers to visualize a home's potential, from furniture to remodeling. This peace of mind can speed up their purchase decision and create interesting opportunities to provide services adjacent to the homebuying process.

If you could solve the biggest challenge on your plate right now, what would that challenge be and why?
Quadrupling the available data scientists and engineers in today's talent pool. We are building the most accurate home pricing model in the industry; that pricing model is tailored to the nuance of every market in which we

operate. That makes hiring top engineering and data science talent a top priority as we look to bring Opendoor to every homeowner in the U.S.

If you achieved your vision for Opendoor, how would the industry be different?

In a world where it is simple and stress-free to sell, buy and manage the responsibilities of owning a home, homeowners will have a greater sense of freedom and peace of mind. We will see more transactions as consumers feel empowered with information and options on how to easily sell or buy. Consumers will also more likely live in homes that actually fit their family's needs, whether it is a smaller home after their kids fly the coop or a larger home that fits a growing family. Ultimately, the industry will be more transparent and easier to navigate.

How will real estate agents' roles change, if at all, in five years?

The agent's role as a consultative expert helping consumers move on to the next chapter in their lives will remain the same. How agents serve their clients will change. The industry has already seen the benefit of technology-enabled services such as DocuSign (docusign.com), which has allowed agents to deliver a better client experience.

We will continue to see advances in technologies and services that improve agent workflow, remove friction in transactions and provide more options that better meet consumers' specific needs. There will be a shift away from time-consuming tasks that limit agent activity, enabling agents to spend more time on the consultative parts of the process that clients value most.

Glenn Kelman, Redfin CEO

Kelman has led Redfin (redfin.com) as its CEO since 2005 and has grown it into a national brand, a Wall Street darling and a $2 billion valuation. Prior to joining Redfin in 2005, Kelman worked in various leadership

About Redfin

Since 2006, Redfin has used technology to provide brokerage services to buyers and sellers at a discount of traditional commissions (read more about Redfin and the emerging brokerage model it uses in Trend No. 3, "Rise of the Modern Discount Brokerage.") In July 2017, Redfin went public raising $138 million, and in the process exposed details of its business model and operations to the industry.

roles at the portal software company Plumtree Software, which he co-founded in 1997 and helped guide toward an initial public offering in 2002.

Note: The Swanepoel Trends Report editorial team selected Glenn Kelman to write the foreword for this year's report. Previous edition forewords have been written by Gary Keller (Founder of Keller Williams Realty), Richard Smith (Chairman and CEO of Realogy Holdings), Bob Moline (CEO of HomeServices of America), Dale Stinton (CEO of NAR), and Spencer Rascoff (CEO of Zillow Group).

The firm is growing quickly. From 2014 to 2016, its annual transaction sides more than doubled from 12,688 sides to 25,686 sides. The company lost double-digit millions each of those three years, but the losses decreased as a percentage of overall revenue from 19.7 percent in 2014 to 8.4 percent in 2016, as shown in its financial statements. In third quarter 2017, it reported a net profit of $10.6 million.

Redfin Overview

Timeline	Founded in 2004, launched in 2006, expanded nationally in 2015, went public on July 28, 2017.
Product/Service	Technology-focused discount brokerage that provides full service for listing fees of 1.5 percent (1 percent in over 20 markets) and buyer rebates, which averaged $3,500 in 2016.
Growth	From 2014 to 2016, the brokerage roughly doubled its annual transaction side count and annual sales volume to 25,868 and $16.2 billion, respectively.
Scope/Scale	84 markets in all 50 states.

How do you think Redfin will significantly or fundamentally change homebuying or the real estate industry?
One of Redfin's goals is to ensure that brokerages get more traffic to their listings. Consumers can connect directly with an agent who can answer their questions about a home and the cost for agents to meet customers can decline over time.

How certain are you that this change will take place within five years? What percentage of brokerages and agents will feel the impact within that timeframe?
We are certain that this change will take place; it is just a matter of degree. The goal is not a revolution; the goal is a modest increase in consumer traffic to brokerage sites, with some fraction of homebuyers contacting agents directly rather than through an advertising site. Since internet traffic increases each year, there should be plenty of business to go around for everyone.

Which technology or company, other than Redfin, will also significantly change the real estate industry within five years?
We think MLSs will reassert themselves to make IDX work better for large brokerages who mostly control MLSs, and to ensure the listing brokerages also get fair attribution from the portals for their listings.

Opendoor and OfferPad are also interesting. The question is whether a shift from a seller's market to a buyer's market will make homeowners more price-sensitive and favor the agent-mediated sale offered by traditional brokerages over one by these emerging players. However, it is also possible that such a market shift will make sellers more convenience-driven or risk-averse, which would favor the experience offered by Opendoor and OfferPad. Time will tell.

If you could solve the biggest challenge on your plate right now, what would that challenge be and why?
The industry's biggest challenge is the quality of contacts from internet search sites, including Redfin. The software engineers building these sites have optimized them to generate more contacts, largely without knowing which ones lead to sales. Agents handling those contacts then have to sort through who is most likely to buy a house.

The result has often been a degradation of service, where agents get overwhelmed with customer contacts or limit the effort they put into each contact. As an industry, we have not really figured out how to close the loop between search sites and the agents who deliver service. It is a broken customer experience, and it is exhausting and frustrating for agents.

How will real estate agents' roles change, if at all, in five years?
Agents will focus more on delivering stellar service to create repeat and referral business rather than prospecting. Listers will last. There will be more top producers and fewer agents overall. Technology will make real estate more efficient, but rather than just lowering prices it will sometimes result in higher levels of service.

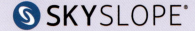

Tyler Smith, SkySlope CEO and Founder
A former top-producing real estate agent and a 2011 Realtor Magazine "30 Under 30" honoree, Smith built SkySlope (skyslope.com) from the

About SkySlope
SkySlope has grown into one of the industry's most prominent transaction management platforms since its launch in 2009. The Sacramento, California-based firm's digital platform allows brokerages and their agents to manage, process, complete and collaborate on transactions online. Its client roster of over 1,500 brokerages include some of the nation's largest such as Howard

ground up with a real estate practitioner's sensibility. Before running SkySlope full-time as its CEO, Smith ran a real estate team that closed nearly 700 transactions and over $200 million in annual sales volume.

Hanna (howardhanna.com), Alain Pinel Realtors (apr.com), Realty One Group (realtyonegroup.com) and Pacific Union International (pacificunion.com) (SkySlope doesn't sell directly to agents). In the last year, it began offering its clients transaction coordination services. In October 2017, title service giant Fidelity National Financial (fnf.com) acquired a majority interest in the company.

SkySlope Overview

Timeline	Founded in 2009, released digital signature tool DigiSign in 2012, introduced transaction coordination service SkyTC in 2015, has grown significantly and sold a majority stake to Fidelity in October 2017.
Product/Service	Digital transaction management platform and transaction coordination service for brokerages and their agents.
Growth	More than doubled employee count in 2016 from 41 to 96 and moved to a new 24,000-square-foot headquarters, quadrupling its previous size.
Scope/Scale	1,500 brokerage clients and 140,000 agents doing 1.5 million transactions each year. Serves 53 of the top 100 U.S. brokerages ranked by sides or sales volume.

How do you think SkySlope will change significantly or fundamentally change homebuying or the real estate industry?
SkySlope is automating the real estate industry. Think Tesla (tesla.com). Think self-driving cars. We are building the technology that will make transactions self-driving so that agents can focus on their clients, on building relationships and on growing their business. The way real estate operates will be entirely different, and everyone in real estate will benefit: homebuyers and sellers, service providers, brokers and agents.

How certain are you that this change will take place within five years? What percentage of brokerages and agents will feel the impact within that timeframe?
Five years is a long time when it comes to the speed of technology evolution. A large amount of capital has poured into the real estate space. Investors are making big bets and looking to disrupt; when that happens, industries shift quickly.

I'm 100 percent certain that complete automation will take place within five years. Automation will be the new standard and agents who do not adapt to it are going to fall behind because the consumer will come to expect it.

SkySlope is already utilizing machine-learning and our broker clients and agents are taking advantage of this technology within the SkySlope application. We have just gotten started and already we are seeing huge benefits. In five years, we will have complete automation. All pieces of the process will integrate and flow with automation, and it likely will extend far beyond transaction management.

Which technology or company, other than SkySlope, will also significantly change the real estate industry within five years?
I am keeping my eye on Amazon (amazon.com). I know it seems unrelated, but Amazon is starting to dabble in home-related products and services. I would not be shocked to see them step into the real estate space.

At this point, it is hard to imagine, but it was also hard to imagine Airbnb (airbnb.com, letting strangers stay in your home for a weekend) or Uber (uber.com, click a button to request a ride). So, while it may sound crazy, it is not unreasonable to consider Amazon entering the real estate industry and shaking things up.

If you could solve the biggest challenge on your plate right now, what would that challenge be and why?
Having been an agent, I understand the process of serving clients and I want to build technology that automates and eliminates the pain points. I want to expand on automated transactions so they become self-driving, leaving no work for the agent – the paperwork all but fills out itself.

I would also love for agents and brokers to embrace technology because it exists to help them. Technology allows real estate professionals to build relationships with their clients. The highest and best use of an agent's time involves spending time with clients, managing their emotions and exceeding their expectations. Technology will take care of everything else.

How will real estate agents' roles change, if at all, in five years?
The real estate process is incredibly complicated, but it does not have to be. Agents can focus on the fundamentals of buying and selling homes and building trust with their clients.

That said, the future will include far fewer agents. The agents who focus on efficiency and value will thrive. The traditional model will evolve. Agents' roles will be less archaic. They will not need transaction skills. Of course, they will need to understand contracts, but the skills of sales, relationship-building and market expertise will trump all.

Errol Samuelson, Zillow Group Chief Industry Development Officer

Errol Samuelson has played a significant role in real estate's technology revolution, first as president of Move Inc.'s customer relationship management platform Top Producer Systems from 2003 to 2007, then as president of realtor.com from 2007 until March 2014 when he joined Zillow Group (zillowgroup.com) as Chief Industry Development Officer. In his current role, he oversees Zillow Group's business-to-business product development and tools, which include a comprehensive listing management platform for brokerages and MLSs, a mortgage pricing engine and digital transaction management platform dotloop (dotloop.com).

About Zillow Group

Since its launch in 2006 with automated Zestimate home valuations, Zillow Group has pushed the industry forward with its unrelenting focus on innovation and serving consumers' best interests. After acquiring chief rival Trulia in February 2015 for $2.5 billion, Zillow Group became the U.S.'s dominant real estate portal. Its flagship site zillow.com attracted 23.2 million unique visitors in October, just over twice that of its chief competitor realtor.com, according to the Hitwise division of Connexity (estimate does not include mobile app traffic). Over 80,000 real estate agents pay Zillow Group for ZIP code-based access to this vast audience, which helped put the company on pace to generate over $1 billion in 2017. In addition to its dominant New York City portal StreetEasy (streeteasy.com) and millennial-focused site RealEstate.com, the firm operates a growing rentals business under the brands HotPads (hotpads.com) and Naked Apartments (nakedapartments.com).

Zillow Group Overview

Timeline	Founded in 2006, raised $75 million while going public in 2011, acquired Trulia and dotloop in 2015, acquired MLS technology provider Bridge Interactive Group in 2016, projected to record over $1 billion in revenues in 2017
Product/ Service	Advertising, leads and technology for real estate agents and brokers; brokerage and MLS technology provider; rental professional technology and advertising provider.
Growth	Annual revenue increase of over 25 percent based on mid-point of projected 2017 revenue of $1.06 billion.
Scope/Scale	Over 80,000 agent advertisers, owner of real estate's largest consumer audience by a wide margin.

How do you think Zillow Group will significantly or fundamentally change homebuying or the real estate industry?
We are focused on creating a marketplace that connects consumers (buyers, sellers, renters and homeowners) with professionals (agents, brokers, property managers, mortgage brokers and investors). By providing transparency and addressing consumer needs, we now capture the largest consumer audience in real estate on desktop and mobile.

But our goals go beyond making connections. We are working to help real estate brokers, agents and other professionals streamline the buying and selling process. We also help property managers and individual real estate investors reduce the friction in the rental process.

With what results?
We believe that within five years, real estate transactions will be completely digital. Consumers will have better visibility, certainty and predictability around transactions. They will also have a greater sense of control, leading to higher satisfaction. Agents and teams will become more productive as a result of working with empowered consumers and leveraging technology. As pain points fade and transaction certainty and predictability increase, we may well see more transactions occur – the size of the real estate pie could grow. Brokerages who embrace end-to-end digital transactions will see their margins improve; others will continue to face margin pressure.

Which technology or company, other than Zillow Group, will also significantly change the real estate industry within five years?
We are watching the following three trends.

Consumers' expectations of speed and convenience: Nearly half of all homebuyers are first-time buyers (and 42 percent of buyers are millennials). Nearly two-thirds of sellers have never sold a home before. Online experiences shape these real estate buyers' and sellers' expectations. In 45 cities, they can get two-hour delivery via Amazon Prime Now; they expect their real estate agent to respond faster than that. Buyers and sellers are also willing to trade money for convenience. Almost a third of millennials grocery shop online, even though online prices can be 25 percent higher than at traditional stores. These new buyers and sellers expect real-time service and transparency, and are willing to pay a premium for convenience. These demands will further accelerate the agent team trend and will require agents and brokers to adopt end-to-end technology. These new consumers are more focused on service and convenience than they are on commission rates.

Challenges of nonwhite real estate consumers: Buyers and sellers are becoming more diverse. Nearly half of millennials are nonwhite; since 2010, Hispanics have accounted for 60 percent of homeownership growth. Unfortunately, many barriers to homeownership for nonwhites exist, including access to credit. For example, when applying for a conventional loan, black applicants and Hispanic applicants are 2.6 times and two times more likely to be denied, respectively, than Caucasian applicants. If we want to have a healthy real estate industry in 2022, we need to rapidly address the underlying issues that make it difficult for nonwhites to access homeownership.

Artificial intelligence and machine learning: Artificial intelligence (AI) and machine learning will have a huge impact on all industries and society as a whole. Within real estate, we are already seeing AI improve search, recommendations and the consumer experience. For example, at Zillow Group we use machine vision to improve our Zestimates by analyzing property photos to determine home finishes, appliances and more. But the real impact of AI will come from its effects on society. The autonomous economy is steadily digesting the physical economy and the jobs it provides, according to renowned economist W. Brian Arthur.

In short, the housing market will no longer be "business as usual" in five years. All players will need to be nimble and responsive.

If you could convince brokerage leaders of one thing, what would it be?
The most important thing brokers can provide their agents is a strong culture, based on well-understood, shared core values. Structure and coaching to reinforce these values and establish accountability are critical in helping agents truly live company culture.

If you achieved your vision for Zillow Group, how would the industry be different?
The uncertainty and angst experienced by consumers during the buying, selling and renting process will significantly diminish. Transactions will be more transparent, more predictable, less complex and even exciting and aspirational. By removing the barriers and friction that consumers experience today, we may even see people deciding to move more frequently – actually expanding the real estate market. Also, there will be more choice and opportunity for homeowners of all races and ethnicities. Agents, agent teams and brokerages will continue to be integral in helping consumers through the process.

How will real estate agents' roles change, if at all, in five years?
Agents will continue functioning as essential elements in the real estate transaction. In fact, I think the percentage of consumers using an agent will increase. Having said that, many consumers will become more involved in all aspects of the transaction, including search, discovery, price setting, merchandising their home and even in negotiations. Consumers will play a more active role in choosing their mortgage and title providers, and they will do more research prior to selecting their professional advisors.

Agents will continue to provide tremendous value: helping consumers understand the transaction, identifying potential pitfalls, keeping the process moving, providing counsel and decision support, and helping identify necessary professionals (legal resources, inspectors, etc.). Agents will also continue to give insight on the context of a home, such as what a neighborhood is like and how will it change over the next five years. And agent teams will be able to provide seamless service and specialized support. Finally, brokers will provide an environment that enables agents and teams to thrive, and will be appropriately compensated.

Michael Bruce, Purplebricks Founder and Global CEO

A lawyer by training, Michael Bruce and his younger brother Kenny owned and served as managing director for the regional U.K. real estate brokerage Burchell Edwards Group (burchelledwards.co.uk) and its conveyancing firm before selling it to U.K. real estate brokerage giant Connells Group in 2011. He and Kenny then went to work on the concept that led to Purplebricks (purplebricks.com): a technology-based real estate brokerage that provides U.K. sellers full service at a fraction of the cost of traditional firms.

About Purplebricks

Purplebricks offers a technology-focused discount brokerage model aided by big marketing spends and local agent representation. Instead of the typical 1.5 percent listing commission U.K. agents charge (buyer agency does not exist in the U.K.), Purplebricks, which has no brick-and-mortar offices, lists and markets homes for a flat fee of approximately $1,148. Based on the average U.K. home sales price of $299,464 in July 2017, this represents savings of $3,344, or 74 percent compared to a traditional commission rate. The company went public on the London Stock Exchange in December 2015, expanded to Australia in August 2016 and the U.S. in September 2017. In October 2017, the company's market cap was over $1.3 billion, more than triple that of its public U.K. brokerage rivals Countrywide (countrywide.co.uk), Foxtons Group (foxtonsgroup.co.uk) and LSL Property Services (lslps.co.uk), whose market caps were $358 million, $238 million and $319 million, respectively.

Purplebricks raised $62 million through a special stock offering in early 2017 to bring its model to the U.S. It opened its first location in Los Angeles in September 2017 with plans to expand throughout California before launching nationwide. The firm adapted its model to fit the U.S. market, primarily by accommodating buyer agency. However, the business model is essentially unchanged: Purplebricks continues to offer a technology platform that facilitates buyer and seller self-service, local independent contractor agent representation, heavy brand marketing, no brokerage offices and flat fees. In Los Angeles, Purplebricks lists homes for a flat fee of $3,200, which the seller pays regardless of whether the home sells. Sellers can defer payment for up to six months if the home does not sell. The company rebates $1,000 of the buy-side commission to its buyers upon close. It offers market-rate buy-side commission to buyer agents on its listings.

Purplebricks Overview

Timeline	Founded in 2012, launched in 2014, went public in December 2015, expanded to Australia in August 2016 and California in September 2017.
Product/Service	Technology-focused real estate brokerage with in-house agents providing full service to consumers at a steep discount to traditional real estate.
Growth	In fiscal year 2016, it more than doubled its year-over-year U.K. sales volume and agent count to $7.8 billion and 448, respectively.
Scope/Scale	Has become one of the U.K.'s largest brokerages, is growing fast in Australia and entered the U.S. in September 2017.

How do you think Purplebricks will significantly or fundamentally change homebuying or the real estate industry?
The real estate industry is ripe for change. Traditional brokerage firms are finding themselves at a standstill and are using old methods to generate new business. For instance, we at Purplebricks have capitalized on the appetite for a transformation. We recognized the opportunity to offer customers a convenient, transparent and cost-effective solution enabling them to see and know what is happening 24/7.

Our particular model also offers customers full support by local agents we call "Local Real Estate Experts" and a team of professionals who consumers and clients can contact at any time. The ability to arrange a valuation, book a showing or tour, give feedback, make an offer – all digitally – gives customers greater insight into the process, something they crave. The biggest investment we can make, as leaders in the real estate industry, is in our customers. Giving them a technology- and people-based solution will change the way transactions are conducted. We believe our proven model is game-changing and will have a positive effect on the overall industry.

How certain are you that this change will take place within five years? What percentage of brokerages and agents will feel the impact within that timeframe?
Our business model has enjoyed immense success in both the U.K. and Australia after just several years in each market. Through extensive,

on-the-ground research, we now have an office in Los Angeles, and we are planning to expand across the U.S. We see the changes in the worldwide market regarding the way real estate transactions are done.

Customers want greater insight into the real estate process. They do not want to sit back and wait. Whether buying or selling, they want everything to be available instantly, which technology enables. If you have access to everything you need to know at the touch of a button, much of the stress that accompanies the homebuying and selling process melts away, helping consumers make better, more-informed decisions.

We believe we are at the forefront of a technological and consumer advancement. Our feeling is that five years down the line, there will be far less physical real estate offices and more of a virtual and digital landscape. The need for agents to sit in an office and wait for customers to visit will be few and far between – they will be in their respective markets using the technology at their fingertips. We feel good about the direction the market is taking and are pleased that our company is leading this new trend.

Which technology or company, other than Purplebricks, will also significantly change the real estate industry within five years?
We see virtual reality playing a much more significant role in the overall buyer experience. This goes back to transacting with the touch of a button. For instance, one could ideally "walk the halls" of a home – in a more multi-sensory, information-rich experience than VR can offer today – to get a feel for what living in this particular space offers without having to physically be there.

If you could convince brokerage leaders of one thing, what would it be?
To embrace technology and to understand that doing so does not mean there is not a need for people. Real estate will always be a people business. As technology continues to develop, transactions become more seamless, lead generation improves and real estate agents find themselves with more time to service more customers. Why would we not want to embrace something that will aid our efficiency?

How will real estate agents' roles change, if at all, in five years?
Technology will help real estate agents deliver a better, more reliable and convenient service. They will earn more money because they will be more productive. We at Purplebricks have streamlined the agent role, made it faster, more reliable and, more importantly, totally focused on servicing customers. We believe more and more traditional brokerage models will adopt new ways to operate. We are on the frontline of change. In five years, this industry will be a more oiled machine and customers worldwide will benefit hugely.

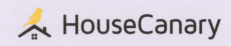

Jeremy Sicklick, HouseCanary Co-Founder and CEO
Before co-founding HouseCanary (housecanary.com) in 2014, Sicklick earned an MBA from The Wharton School in 2002 and worked as a management consultant, most recently at The Boston Consulting Group as partner and managing director. The Great Recession and the lack of high-quality housing data and accurate valuation models inspired Sicklick and Chris Stroud to co-found the company.

About HouseCanary
HouseCanary crunches thousands of pieces of data to create automated home valuations on 100 million U.S. homes. It uses big data, machine learning and artificial intelligence to refine its algorithms. The firm offers appraisal software and data to appraisers, market data reports to brokers and agents, valuation and predictive analytics to real estate investors of all sizes, and valuations to lenders. The firm raised $64 million in 2017 to pour gas on its goal to bring its valuation technology to more real estate brokers, agents and consumers.

HouseCanary Overview

Timeline	Founded in 2014, the San Francisco office opened in 2015, announced $33 million Series A round in January 2017, opened a Boulder, Colorado, office in June 2017, announced $31 million Series B round in September 2017.
Product/Service	Uses big data, machine learning and artificial intelligence to create automated home valuations.
Growth	Has roughly doubled its employee count in the last year from less than 50 to over 100 as of October 2017. The nation's largest owner of single-family rental homes, Blackstone's Invitation Homes, is a client.
Scope/Scale	Offers full data coverage in 381 metro areas, 17,000 ZIP codes over 3 million residential blocks and 100 million homes.

How do you think HouseCanary will significantly or fundamentally change homebuying or the real estate industry?
Buying real estate is a lengthy, cumbersome process. Buyers typically search for 10 weeks, according to the National Association of Realtors 2016 Profile of Home Buyers and Sellers. The mortgage process in particular is slow and stressful. On average, it takes over 40 days from loan application day to close, according to Ellie Mae data.

The appraisal process – the task of valuing homes accurately – is a major reason for delays. On average, appraisals take from 20 to 30 days to complete, and in high-demand areas they can take as long as six to eight weeks.

HouseCanary addresses these appraisal hurdles with its highly accurate automated valuations with extremely low error rates (2.5 percent median absolute error) thanks to big data and artificial intelligence. When human-in-the-loop inspections or appraisals are required, our technology will allow them to happen much faster; instead of weeks, it will take hours.

How certain are you that this change will take place within five years? What percentage of brokerages and agents will feel the impact within that timeframe?
I am very confident this will take place within five years. Artificial intelligence and big data allow us to value a hundred million U.S. properties with accuracy. Appraisal technology will remove tedious aspects of human appraisals and allow appraisers to focus instead on fine-tuning automated valuation inputs. This is already happening, and it will only get better and faster.

Which technology or company, other than HouseCanary, will also significantly change the real estate industry within five years?
Notarize (notarize.com) will help speed up mortgage transactions by allowing borrowers to electronically sign and notarize the entire loan package online. It does most of this already by connecting borrowers with a notary over a live video call; the notary walks the parties through the signing process and legally notarizes the closing package.

But we think technology, rather than an individual company, will likely have more impact. The democratization of artificial intelligence and machine learning by the nation's largest companies such as Google (google.com), Amazon, Microsoft (microsoft.com) and Apple (apple.com) are developing technology such as image classification and annotation, data collection and categorization, object classification, natural language processing, chatbots, and pricing and risk modeling that have powerful real estate applications.

If you could convince brokerage leaders of one thing, what would it be?
Increase access to data. One of the biggest challenges in the real estate industry is the fragmented nature of data (e.g. MLS data, public records, listing data). This impedes innovation as it stifles companies who want to develop tools to help agents become better advisors and be better at their day-to-day jobs.

How will real estate agents' roles change, if at all, in five years?
In five years, buyers and sellers will be more data-driven in selecting the right agent. In response, agents will be more data-driven as well in finding buyer and seller prospects, setting the right price for a property, engaging their sphere of influence and more.

COMPASS

Robert Reffkin, Compass Co-Founder and CEO

Robert Reffkin has overseen whirlwind, well-funded growth as CEO of Compass (compass.com). In many ways, he embodies real estate's technology and venture capital revolution. While he had an impressive resume before co-founding Compass in 2012, including stints as chief of staff for the chief operating officer of Goldman Sachs and as a White House Fellow, Reffkin had not worked in organized real estate before co-founding Compass in 2012. Six years and $775 million of venture funding later, he has led New York City-based Compass into a national force with over 2,000 agents in 40 offices in 11 markets and a valuation of $2.2 billion.

About Compass

Compass exemplifies the effect venture capital has had on real estate in recent years. Launched in 2012, it has grown to over 2,000 agents and a national brand with the help of a steady stream of venture funding. The firm promises agents and consumers the brokerage of the future and has invested in the human and tech resources to make good on that goal; software engineers and product-focused staff make up 25 percent of its 500 full-time employees. Its tech platform gives agents personalized recommendations and insights on how to better serve their clients, data-borne insights into how to optimize their business, a digital marketing center that facilitates the creation of sleek marketing pieces, and a search tool that allows them to collaborate with clients on their searches. In conjunction with its November 2017 funding round, the firm announced plans to expand to an additional 10 markets and grow market share in existing markets to 20 percent. In December, it closed a game-changing $450 million round to fuel that vision.

Compass Overview

Timeline	Launched in 2012, closed $25 million in venture funding in 2013, expanded to Washington, D.C., and raises $42 million in 2014. Grew to 500 agents and raised $60 million in 2015, agent count surpassed 1,000 and reached $1 billion valuation with a $90 million raise in 2016. Grew agent count and raised a game-changing $550 million for a $2.2 billion valuation in 2017.
Product/ Service	High-end branding, marketing and technology support for agents. Has an in-house CRM platform with listings, client and transaction data for agents and clients.
Growth	Doubled agent count every year since 2015, including 2017, which saw its agent corps count top 2,000.
Scope/Scale	Has 40 offices in 11 high-end markets across the country with announced plans to launch 10 new markets by 2020.

What technology do you think will change (significantly or fundamentally) homebuying or the real estate industry the most within the next five years?
We believe artificial intelligence (AI) will transform every industry, including real estate. By harnessing the data that underpins the real estate industry, we will be able to apply AI to give agents incredible competitive advantages, including the ability to provide real-time market insights and recommendations to clients.

Data in the real estate industry is extremely fragmented. Aggregating and translating this data into powerful insights for individual agents and clients is extremely challenging, but that is the most exciting opportunity to create a new future. We are building an integrated platform with listings, client and transaction data all in one place that will be able to deliver these data driven insights and recommendations.

How certain are you that this change will take place within five years (so end of 2022)? What percentage of brokerages and agents will feel the impact within that timeframe?
These changes are taking place even now and I expect that by 2022 we will see widespread implications of technology, and AI specifically. Agents who adopt technology and brokerages that invest in it will have a significant competitive advantage over those who do not. The best agents, armed with AI and data-driven technology, will do 10 times the transaction volume they do today. Brokerages who do not provide their agents with powerful tools and leveraging data to help their agents grow their business will find it harder and harder to retain the best agents. In five years, all agents and brokerages will feel the impact of AI and data-driven technology.

If you could convince agents of one thing, what would it be?
If I could convince agents of one thing, it would be that they are in control of their own destiny. Agents should think of themselves as CEOs and ensure they have the support — or a team to help them — with budgeting, branding, marketing, hiring and developing talent, strategic planning and goal-setting.

If you could solve the biggest challenge on your plate right now, what would that challenge be, why?
I would love to be able to hire more data and AI experts so we can move even faster in executing our vision to empower agents through technology.

If you achieved your vision for Compass, how would the industry be different?
Real estate agents will be considered a highly respected advisory profession, much like wealth managers or lawyers. In the future, people graduating from the top colleges in the country will aspire to become real estate agents.

How will real estate agents' roles change, if at all, in five years?
In an AI-powered future, the role of the agent will be focused on sharing insights and providing a high-touch experience, which is fundamentally all about relationship-building, listening and providing experienced counsel.

Takeaway

Consumers and agents empowered by technology and the options they present is a clear theme through these Q&As. A second is the belief that artificial intelligence and machine learning will have a huge impact on the industry with respect to automation, new big data-driven insights, products and services. Complete or almost complete digital transactions will speed up the homebuying and selling process, potentially facilitate more home sales and hopefully reduce duplication and waste. That, of course, is an enormous vision.

Everyone agrees that agents will be essential components of the industry's future, but their roles will increasingly shift toward that of counselors, advisors and project managers rather than data gatekeepers or providers. Agents will have more time to serve clients as technology increasingly removes the mundane tasks that can be easily automated with computer vision and increasingly integrated systems. The challenge, of course, is that these changes alter agents' value propositions and their jobs, potentially limiting the industry's agent count and the number of those who can make healthy livings as full-time agents.

The Swanepoel Trends Report will continue to thoroughly evaluate and analyze all these shifts before they occur.

Note:
None of the companies or leaders included in this report approached T3 Sixty. Inclusion decisions were made solely by our editorial team and based on a desire to get these leaders' insights. We designed the questions to elicit specific information about their organizations and to expand and extend the forward-thinking dialogue the Swanepoel Trends Report fosters.

09

The Complex World of Commerical Real Estate

Emerging Trends

With a global value measured in the trillions of dollars, commercial real estate drives vast segments of the U.S. economy at the local, national and international levels. At the same time, it impacts the value of residential real estate as development and the construction of commercial and residential buildings largely determine the future distribution of job and housing locations. Just as e-commerce, demographic trends, changing consumer habits and technology are reshaping residential real estate, these forces are transforming the commercial industry. In 2017, T3 Sixty completed and published on behalf of the National Association of Realtors, a study titled the Commercial Real Estate ALERT Report (Analysis of the Latest Emerging Risks and Trends). What follows is an adapted extract from that report.

Forces Shaping Commercial Real Estate

Commercial real estate (CRE) touches nearly every segment of the economy. In some industries it plays a significant role and includes office-oriented businesses, retail, distribution, leisure and public infrastructure. Because of its core role in the economy, business trends have an outsized effect on it. Some of these include rapidly evolving technology, major demographic shifts and increasing urbanization.

Commercial property located close to residential developments can impact both sale and rental prices, especially properties located near large commercial developments. For example, the suburbs were booming in the 1950s as people moved out of core urban centers into newly developed residential neighborhoods. In turn, the suburbs became commercial centers of shopping malls and office buildings to meet the needs of suburban residents. But over time, with the emergence of Generation X and millennials, the move away from urban centers reversed itself with a move back to urban areas for closer proximity to work, shopping, and the amenities that are a key part of their live-work-play lifestyle.

Residential and commercial real estate face many of the same change agents: the rise of e-commerce, changing consumer habits and expectations, a deepening digital revolution, aging leadership with not many successors in sight and huge capital investments from outside sources. Commercial faces some unique changes as well including the rise of demand for sustainable buildings, the shifting demand for warehouse areas and the way retail works and the complexity of international financing. In this chapter, we take a brief look at the following key issues.

- **The Need for Capital** – Global Access Opens New Opportunities
- **The New Crowd** – A New Alternative Financing Avenue
- **Technology and Big Data** – Game-changers for CRE
- **A New Direction** – E-Commerce Impacting CRE
- **New Faces** – New Places – Emerging Millennials and Retiring Boomers
- **Sustainability** – The Problem of ROI
- **A Deeper Look** – Commercial Real Estate ALERT

> "The commercial real estate business is a bottom-line business. Period."

The Need for Capital

Global Access Opens New Opportunities

CRE enters 2018 with concerns about the impact global volatility and instability may have on the industry. A few of the unknowns include a global currency weakening in the face of a stronger U.S. dollar, low energy prices, conflicting monetary policies, an uncertain economy in China and the European Union dealing with Brexit. On the domestic scene, continued uncertainty abounds around the direction of government policy over the next few years.

These issues cast a shadow of uncertainty over the economy. A leading concern is whether the healthy flow of cross-border capital that has helped CRE enjoy five consecutive years of double-digit returns will continue. The question facing the industry is whether or not this investment pattern will persist in the midst of growing global issues, record high property prices and investors hesitating until they see what direction the U.S. takes. As a result, interest has grown in markets outside the prime gateway markets of New York City, Los Angeles, Washington, D.C., Chicago, and Boston.

The Move to Secondary Markets

With interest rates low and the economy showing overall strength and growth, many anticipate that CRE will enjoy even greater inflows of foreign capital in the years ahead. However, unlike the past, a significant share of that investment will come from a growing third wave of investors: insurance companies and private equity funds following the lead of sovereign wealth funds and high-net-worth individuals.

While investors have historically focused on prime properties in gateway markets, investment opportunities have dwindled in those markets, driving them to expand into newer opportunities in secondary and even tertiary markets where they are taking on additional risk to improve returns. This follows a change in investment strategy from primarily focusing on capital preservation to a focus on income-producing, yield-focused opportunities. These secondary markets meet those requirements by offering lower barriers to entry, higher capitalization rates and fundamentals that generally improve as the economy grows.

Foreign Investment

Commercial Real Estate Acquisition by Share of Foreign Investment

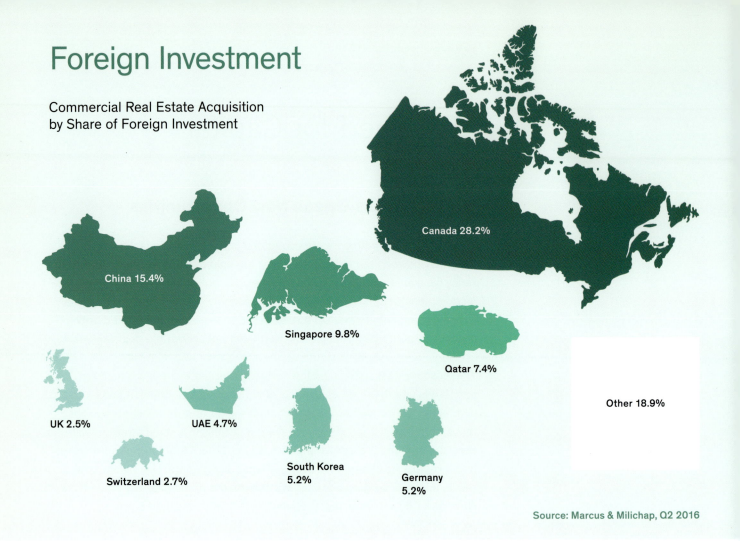

Source: Marcus & Milichap, Q2 2016

Investment in Infrastructure and Energy

Commercial development in 2015 supported 3.2 million jobs in the U.S., contributed $450 billion to the U.S. gross domestic product and developed 429.4 million square feet of space with the capacity to house 1.1 million new workers, according to the National Association for Industrial and Office Properties (NAIOP). The group expects accelerated construction spending with gains in fixed investment in commercial property – office retail, healthcare, distribution facilities and multifamily housing – to accommodate any local labor force increase.

While many CRE industry professionals anticipate that the flow of foreign capital from oil-producing countries may slow, the overall flow of capital from non-oil-producing countries will likely continue and may increase as investors look for opportunities to increase the yield on their capital. If the government's plan to achieve energy independence succeeds, CRE will indirectly benefit from an improved and stronger economy from increased development, higher employment and increased wages. All of which will continue to attract foreign capital.

Need for Capital Summary

There has been a major global stockpiling of CRE investment capital over the past several years. In addition, the volume of foreign capital invested in U.S. commercial properties continues at record rates. While global volatility and uncertainty will continue in the near term, experts expect capital flow to increase. Add to this the tax benefits of the recent legislative changes to government programs for foreign investors, the emergence of foreign qualified pension plans and the continued search for a safe haven with solid fundamentals, and the prospects for continued cross-border CRE investment are positive.

"Global commercial real estate is dominated by the U.S. commercial business."

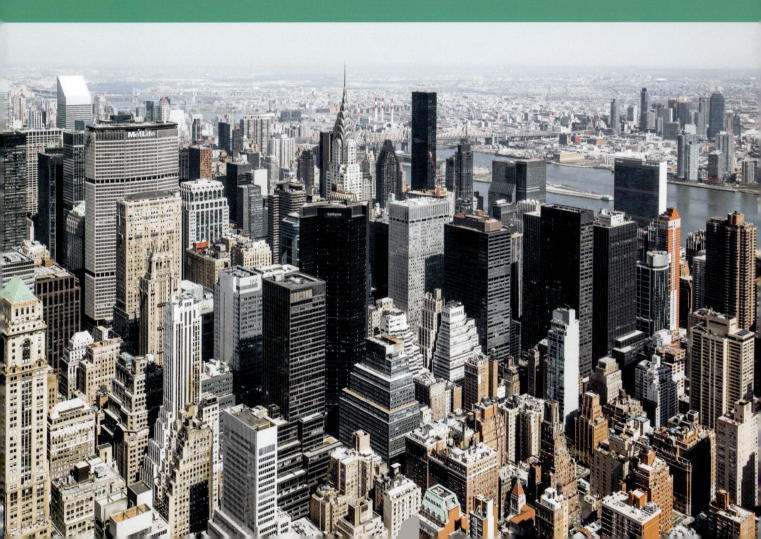

Crowdfunding

A New Financing Avenue

Increased federal regulations have hampered the financial industry's ability to provide sufficient capital to CRE at a time when it lacks development funding. This has forced developers to seek alternate sources of capital such as crowdfunding, a growing avenue for the industry to tap into a vast number of nonaccredited investors for both debt and equity capital.

Crowdfunding (online capital formation) is often referred to as "marketplace lending" or as a "peer-to-peer" portal or platform that gives investors — accredited and nonaccredited — the opportunity to participate in CRE, financially or through equity investments. This relatively new method of financing connects investors with professionally managed properties by pooling their resources online just as investors have done offline through property syndication for decades, but with three key differences:

- **Speed** — By using algorithmic technology, credit decisions and underwriting now happen in minutes, not days.
- **Transparency** — Investors and borrowers gain visibility into the investment, including risks and rewards.
- **Customer-centric** — Crowdfunding portals bring brick-and-mortar investment into the on-demand, smartphone generation.

Crowdfunding portals provide turnkey fundraising and investor management solutions that fulfill U.S. Securities and Exchange Commission requirements by digitally processing required information and investor-funding commitments, managing closings, providing post-closing documentation and streamlining investor communications.

> "Crowdfunding is an innovative new way to get more people investing in commercial real estate."

Investment Options

Investors have two investment options through crowdfunding. Debt shares provide an ownership stake in a mortgage on a property; the investor's return is paid from the interest on the loan. With an investment in the property's equity, the investor shares in a percentage of the rental income and the pass-through tax benefits.

The Negative View

"The important trend question is what sort of economic impact, in the long term, will Social Media and Internet-based platforms, which include crowdfunding, have on CRE?" according to a pension fund manager in the Urban Land Institute's 2016 Emerging Trends in Real Estate report. "I think they'll disintermediate it. Information about specific submarkets and deal sourcing will be dispersed along a lot more quickly. Again, it comes down to scale. Will there be a crowdfunding Zillow? And will large-scale investors be inclined to access such a source for deal making, more than just information gathering?"

Future concerns include how this new source of capital will perform over the real estate cycle and the potential for fraud in a largely unregulated segment of the industry.

The Positive View

Many industry experts believe that raising capital online will become significantly more prevalent in the future. Some even anticipate that by 2025 crowdfunding investments will draw even with private equity financing because regulations complicate small- and mid-sized bank lending.

"Crowdfunding will be the democratization of real estate investment and will scale faster than anyone expects, creating efficiency for private CRE transactions; it's a huge market," according to crowdfunding portal Fundrise (fundrise.com). "What we've seen is, with the decentralized model, it can operate much more efficiently at much cheaper cost. It doesn't have the entire centralized infrastructure that big [bank] branches have with big offices and corporate overhead. I think as you see crowdfunding get larger, and the sums of capital are bigger, I think you're going to see it challenge the existing banking infrastructure, which is very centralized with a lot of overhead and additional costs."

Crowdfunding Summary

The types of equity and debt investors seek through crowdfunding platforms generally do not include assets that traditional CRE lenders typically finance. As a result, financial industry insiders believe that if crowdfunding portals succeed on a larger scale, they will democratize real estate investing. But even if that does not materialize, crowdfunding has opened the door to CRE's $7 trillion market to 98 percent of the potential nonaccredited investors that until now have been all but locked out.

> "Commercial real estate is definitely in vogue and finding good commercial properties is an arduous task."

Technology and Big Data

> "Data is coming at commercial real estate from everywhere."

Game-Changers for CRE

The emergence of big data as a key decision-making tool throughout CRE has forced developers, investors, owners and real estate companies to incorporate technology into their strategic plans to remain competitive in a rapidly evolving, digitally-driven and technology-enhanced world.

A Fundamental Shift

Big data is driving a fundamental shift in CRE. Historically, it was nearly impossible to aggregate and analyze all the data siloed in different sections of enterprise resource planning systems and spreadsheets. But industry players must now analyze property and market data in real time to remain competitive and keep pace with today's rapidly changing and evolving market.

Advances in e-commerce, cloud computing, mobile access and data analytics make this technology shift possible. Furthermore, advanced technology reduces risk, increases efficiency and provides a competitive advantage by enabling better and more informed decisions thanks to multiple data sources, both public and proprietary. Mobile technologies, big data and the internet of things (IoT) are CRE game-changers.

Analytics Make Big Data Meaningful

The collection and analysis of huge amounts of data has become a key factor in every facet of CRE, from how sales, leases, development, financing and investments progress to the development, operation and management of smart buildings. However, big data's ability to drive better decision-making around asset lifecycle, operational costs, sustainability factors and other core CRE business elements is its biggest value.

By analyzing unstructured data, social media, images and a host of textual information, new technology and cloud-computing advances provide granular insight into core business processes that support accurate decision-making. This increased visibility provides developers, investors, owners and brokers the information they need to make accurate decisions. On the operational side, it improves collaboration and efficiency, risk management and mitigation, the process and system standardization of data generation, and the ability to better monitor, improve and accelerate transactions. The ability to drill down and analyze granular market and property data provides investors better risk analysis and management.

The Challenge of Integration

As a new generation of technology-driven individuals moves into CRE, augmented reality, virtual reality and user-driven experiences are rapidly becoming industry norms. However, many companies are not yet fully taking advantage of these new technologies. They struggle with connectivity and access to data because they lack the technology platforms and capabilities that effectively aggregate and manage data; rapid technology evolution and growing amounts of data compound the challenge.

Advances in distributed technology are one of the key drivers behind the successful integration of technology and big data. Distributed technology allows companies to host physical assets in the virtual world in a distributed and near-impossible-to-tamper-with format. One distributed technology that will play an increasingly important role is blockchain, a highly scalable and secure database, the same platform used by Bitcoin. Blockchain technology provides a compelling alternative to the excessive amount of paper and manpower CRE uses today. "This technology will make it possible for every property (everywhere) to have a digital address that contains occupancy, finance, legal, building performance, physical attributes, and a historical record of all transactions," according to the Urban Land Institute.

"Even when it comes to commercial real estate, people still want to see it, feel it, touch it."

"Additionally, the data will be immediately available online and correlatable across all properties. Standard practices that normally involve specialists, like title search, legal, finance, etc., will be less needed or in most cases totally unnecessary. The speed to transact will be shortened from days/weeks/months to minutes or seconds."

The Impact on Investors

A major challenge CRE investors face centers on finding the detailed information they need to efficiently analyze rental income risk to make more effective decisions. Traditionally, they had to rely on other information such as lease data and the tenant's commitment and ability to pay rent throughout the term of the lease. Today, investors are expanding their market reach with the help of technology to drill down into the vast volumes of big data now readily available to more accurately assess rental income risk by better analyzing markets, properties, tenant payment delinquencies, risk scores, late-payment histories and more.

As a result, the expectation for unlimited real-time information has become the norm as investor software programs have advanced the ability to analyze big data, making insights more readily available.

The Impact on Owners

With big data, owners can access data from multiple public and private databases and apply analytics to better analyze risks during the lease-negotiation process and throughout the term of the lease. Technology also transforms the way owners manage buildings through remote sensors and automated data processing that enhance operations, reduce costs and drive higher returns. Smart buildings are here and autonomous vehicles are on the horizon.

- **Smart buildings.** These new buildings employ advanced sensor technology and the Internet of Things (IoT) to enhance operation, returns and value. They allow owners, managers, and tenants to take greater control over their operations. Smart building technology has also increased the role the design and development of intelligent buildings plays in investment decisions as they support market differentiation and value beyond location.

- **Autonomous vehicles.** Experts expect 10 million self-driving cars will be on the road by 2020 and that commercial trucks will be commonplace by 2025. Self-driving cars will heavily impact the development and location of both single-family and multifamily housing as commute time becomes less of a location-determining issue. Self-driving cars will also reduce the demand for parking space. The freed-up space in existing parking garages can be utilized for alternative purposes, offering additional investment and revenue-generating opportunities.

Self-driving trucks will transform industrial logistics by greatly changing how goods move between warehouses, stores and residences. Furthermore, self-driving trucks will lead to larger warehouses located further away from city centers. In tandem with automated unloading warehouse facilities, self-driving trucks will dramatically alter distribution building design and site selection decisions driving warehouses to cheaper, more remote locations.

Technology and Big Data Summary

Technology affects almost every aspect of CRE, from how industry professionals get data, analyze it, manage it and use it to shape every aspect of where we work, how we get there and what we accomplish on the way. Along with the impact of an increasingly mobile and connected workforce, it has already greatly altered the office sector, changing the amount of required floor space, office location, and the design, use and management of offices. Owners are altering office buildings to incorporate technology-enabled networks that provide greater flexibility for both organizations and employees.

A New Direction

E-Commerce Impacting CRE

E-commerce has been steadily growing, invading every part of the economy and now experts expect it to have a significant impact on CRE. As millennials move into the heart of their business careers, their always-connected lifestyles with immediate access to the IoT are influencing the business world. The biggest impact for CRE has been the transformation of the retail industry into a click-and-knock strategy that is not only altering the appearance of retail centers but also driving massive changes in the industrial sector.

Structural Change

The complexity involved in supply chain management now centers on the delivery of goods to consumers at any time and place from any platform. The fast delivery times now promised by retailers directly impact their real estate needs, and the ripple effect is a retail and industrial game-changer.

As e-commerce sales skyrocket, the demand for last-mile distribution points in major cities has grown. CRE has responded by shifting focus away from

"A retailer with $1 billion of in-store sales requires approximately 300,000 to 350,000 square feet of logistics space. But the same retailer would need approximately 1 million square feet of logistics space for $1 billion in e-commerce sales."

existing regional warehouses once built to serve regional retail outlets to developing large distribution centers to match retail's emerging e-commerce reality. This consumer buying shift also brings challenges that require commercial real estate strategies that incorporate technology that facilitates order processing and accounts for costs of new fulfillment and distribution facilities that support rapid response and delivery times.

A Paradigm Shift

To compete, retailers are adapting their online strategies into business models that once focused on malls and strip centers. The transition necessitates a switch from traditional retail to a mix of e-commerce and destination retail that involves reducing the number of retail stores and opening new industrial distribution and fulfillment centers. They face two major challenges with this shift in strategy: refining their inventory and real estate strategies to reach a new customer audience, and adopting new strategies to handle online orders and deliver products to customers from a variety of locations.
As the percentage of online sales continues to grow, retailers are slowly downsizing store count and size and are focusing their fewer stores in key

locations. Approximately 800 department stores, representing roughly 20 percent of all anchor space in U.S. malls, will close over the next few years with many malls following suit, according to an estimate by commercial real estate research firm Green Street Advisors. As a result, major mall owners are increasing their capital investments by adding restaurants and experiential activities not subject to internet competition.

The Old Industrial is the New Retail-Industrial

What has been bad for retail – declining sales, closing stores and decreasing construction – has been a windfall for the industrial sector. A new retail-industrial sector has emerged that places a high demand on close-in modern warehouse space to match the evolution of supply chains that focus on more efficient and faster product distribution.

E-commerce is forcing retailers to rethink their full supply chain strategy from manufacturing to transportation, distribution, sales and fulfillment. With timeframes from online purchase to delivery compressing, the challenge of locating inventory close to final destinations has become a chief driver for delivery center placement. However, locating property close to core urban areas is becoming more difficult and costly, causing retailers to consider smaller suburban buildings that may not be perfectly located but are close enough to satisfy their infill requirements. This increases demand and rents, reduces vacancies, increases absorption rates and the competition for older, obsolete industrial buildings whose locations define their value.

Development Opportunities

E-commerce not only increases the demand for warehouse space, it changes the types of space buyers want. The move toward larger, more technologically advanced facilities is a big opportunity for developers as a significant portion of currently vacant space is not logistically viable for most e-commerce companies.

With competition for sites close to population centers increasing, lease rates, land prices and development costs continue to climb. This presents a major advantage to landowners and developers – as well as owners of older office buildings who are amenable to office-to-warehouse conversions – with properties suitable for development adjacent to urban areas.

New Direction Summary

As the percentage of e-commerce purchases rise, retailers are changing their supply chains. It is now all about last-mile distribution points and next-day (or next-hour) deliveries. Many CRE executives believe that e-commerce is in the middle of a multiyear expansion phase that will continue the uncertainty in real estate markets, and increase the shift away from existing big box retail centers and regional warehouses to the development of destination and entertainment centers and large distribution centers near key metropolitan areas. This frustrates the retail sector but is a windfall for industrial.

> "Millennials are simply young baby boomers with a computer."

New Faces and New Places

Emerging Millennials and Retiring Boomers

The trend of millennials emerging and boomers retiring transforms the way we live, work and virtually everything we touch. This demographic shift deeply impacts CRE, from its urban and suburban makeup, the size and look of office buildings and where and how people shop and receive their purchases. As millennials elect to live in smaller urban units, boomers are beginning to think about downsizing and senior living arrangements.

The Urban/Suburban Challenge

The country's demographic transition creates an enormous housing and office demand, which has spurred new construction and redevelopment. This has led to increased infill in urban areas as the competition for urban core real estate has become extremely competitive. As a result of this high urban demand, developers are turning to blighted or underused spaces where some cities offer development incentives as part of revitalization efforts that improve local business environments and raise tax revenue. Although millennials prefer urban living, rising rents are forcing many of them to consider moving to mid-sized cities and the suburbs. But, increasingly, those suburbs are looking strikingly similar to the urban environments they are leaving.

These new, millennial-friendly suburban communities will be walkable and connected to cities by high-speed or light rail that feeds city-center job growth and cities as employment nodes. But a move to the suburbs is not all about the amenities. The suburbanization trend is fueled primarily by consideration of jobs, marriage and family. Although millennials are putting off marriage and family until later in life than previous generations, they are not putting it off indefinitely. The Urban Land Institute estimates that 75 percent of millennials still plan to get married, and migration statistics indicate that more of them are moving out of cities and into the suburbs than not. Approximately only 30 percent of them currently live in urban areas.

Office Buildings in Transition

Many industry insiders are asking one big question: Can suburban offices make a comeback? Many believe they will, but only if they incorporate the flexibility and collaborative capabilities that millennials desire in their work environment.

Millennials desire community and collaboration in their work environment above all, which translates into the challenge for developers to design and locate mixed-use environments. Millennials do not view the office as a place dedicated to an individual's work. It is a meeting place for a varied group of people to gather, share and collaborate in an open communication and brainstorming environment. They have no need for telephones or desktop computers; they want technology, digital connections and flexibility. The speed of communication and access to information they surround themselves with conflicts with the traditional corporate office layout. As a result, office sizes are shrinking as companies move away from individual offices and cubicles in favor of more collaborative, social environments.

Millennials' preferences for how and where they work have given rise to the growing co-working trend that impacts both new office building design and the retrofitting of existing buildings. Co-working spaces will become more prevalent as demand for flexible workspace increases. As competition and demand increase for shared workspaces, developers need to consider that amenities such as gyms, access to gourmet coffee and sleek lounge spaces will increasingly play a key role in forming a competitive advantage.

Many new buildings are being designed with varied layouts that differ floor by floor to provide maximum tenant flexibility. With the limited availability of urban land to develop new office buildings, and to meet the current demand for office space, developers are gutting old offices with high vacancy rates and redesigning them with flexible areas and open working environments, resembling those popular in the technology industry. Older office buildings that cannot be retrofitted with new floor layouts and technology are being converted to apartments or hotels where younger workers can live.

Multifamily Morphs

Millennial preference for living in mixed-use environments near work – along with a growing boomer interest in the same lifestyle – contributes to high rents in urban locations, which increases apartment development activity that, in turn, will further accelerate population growth in central business districts. These lifestyle preferences also influence apartment design as developers and owners modify plans to incorporate smaller units such as 300- to 400-square-foot micro-apartments and promote apartment-sharing to address affordability. However, as apartment sizes shrink, the need for the

> "Do not disregard the 65 million-strong Gen X generation that has been defined as the middle child. This transition generation is setting the tone for change in business."

> "We need to find better alternatives than commission-based compensation. It's time for a whole new mindset and generation to redesign the industry."

additional amenities tenants view as entitlements increases. For example, owners and developers often now must provide Wi-Fi access throughout the property, larger social common areas with internet-ready big-screen TVs, coffee bars, workout areas and more.

Senior Momentum

Baby boomers have not finished exerting their influence on CRE. In fact, they will push one of the biggest construction booms in CRE history: senior housing. Senior housing now comprises over 50,000 senior living communities, according to the American Senior Housing Association. In addition, CBRE reports that another 50,070 units are under construction in 99 markets, 80 percent of which began coming online in 2016. Furthermore, the need for facilities of five major types will grow substantially in the future:

- **Independent Living Facilities** — for those who do not need assistance with daily living activities.
- **Assisted Living** — for those no longer capable of performing the activities associated with daily living.
- **Memory Care** — for those who have experienced significant memory loss.
- **Nursing Care** — long-term care facilities offering the highest level of services.
- **Continuing Care Retirement Communities** — broad-based, long-term services from independent living to full-service nursing care.

Unlike other classes of CRE, senior projects can be a compelling investment in primary, secondary and even tertiary markets as the investment is more about underlying market demand than location.

The Coming Leadership Shortage

By 2025 CRE will face a shortage of 15,000 to 25,000 qualified leaders without a significant number of younger leaders to replace them, according to NAIOP. As boomers approach retirement and prepare to pass on leadership duties to Gen X, the question of succession arises as the industry faces a major talent shortage of millennial leaders.

The search for mid-level talent in industries across the spectrum creates a highly competitive market, making it difficult to attract qualified candidates, especially in technology and data access and analytics. Commercial brokerages face the challenge of attracting new, salary-focused talent strapped with student debt into a commission-driven industry. However, the industry is beginning to actively develop formal talent management plans to address recruitment, training and retention by focusing on:

- Making improvements to training and leadership development.
- Addressing recruitment techniques, core competency hiring practices, onboarding processes, mentorship, training, career development, performance reviews, employee recognition, compensation practices and year-round team-building activities.
- Creating succession plans for company CEOs, presidents and C-suite positions.
- Identifying, perfecting, training and mentoring high-potential employees.
- Increasing social media use, online resources and pre-graduation recruiting efforts.
- Adopting or changing work-life balance policies, social responsibility policies, environmental practices and new communication strategies to attract and retain millennials by incorporating their preference for an open, flexible work culture.

However, to date little has been done on a CRE-wide basis to seriously recruit new blood into the industry.

New Faces and New Places Summary

CRE faces some daunting challenges ahead as it comes to grip with a changing, multigenerational workforce. The following are three key takeaways from a NAIOP's September 2016 CRE Conference "Megashifts, Real Estate Cycles & Bankable Predictions; Taking CRE Into the Future:"

- **Training:** Between 60 and 70 percent of real estate training will be online and on-demand.
- **Technology:** By 2025, 10 million or more jobs will be lost to robotics; do not be surprised to see many office buildings of less than 250,000 square feet managed remotely.

> "It costs too much to be green. Green will become more popular when it becomes affordable."

- **Retirement:** CRE will face a potential shortage of 15,000 to 25,000 qualified workers per year through 2025.

Millennials are not the primary driver of change but they will be a facilitator and tremendous beneficiary of leading CRE into a whole new world.

Sustainability

ROI Slows Advancement

Since the introduction of the international green building certification program Leadership in Energy and Environmental Design (LEED) to CRE in 2000, a growing number of local, state and federal sustainability regulations have emerged. Subsequently, CRE faces questions around the conservation of energy and water, the emergence of smart buildings and autonomous vehicles, and the role that conservation will play in property valuations. While CRE leaders have acknowledged sustainability as a significant factor affecting both short-term profits and long-term valuation, they tend to view it as an expensive step to attract tenants and satisfy new green regulations that reduce profits. Shareholder return currently drives considerations more than the identification as a green owner.

Sustainability and Value

As sustainability gains regulatory momentum, investors and owners will have to incorporate tougher and more wide-ranging sustainability approaches in their investment and asset-management strategies. They must determine how sustainability performance relates to risk, valuation, tenant retention, depreciation and obsolescence, which directly relate to optimizing the all-important metric of return on investment. While the move toward greater sustainability presents both opportunities and risks to the industry, owners and developers must determine how to implement green protocols that support short-term profitability.

> "Sustainability tastes great, but it is not filling."

While many CRE leaders see sustainability's key benefit as a reduction in costs, the opposite is also true. The failure to incorporate sustainable features in buildings could lead to lower revenues. In some markets, energy-inefficient buildings have already suffered lower rents, or what has become known as a "brown discount."

"Architecture and sustainability are important, but capital and ROI even more."

Gaining Control

Modern energy management systems collect and analyze thousands of data points that provide property managers and engineers real-time insight into how to reduce energy costs. These systems not only deliver visibility into building performance, they offer suggestions for how to optimize energy consumption and reduce costs.

CRE is slowly transitioning from traditional database management systems toward real-time predictive analysis and cloud-based meter management that provide real-time energy consumption feedback. A focused program can provide owners with an immediate understanding of how reducing energy and utility costs impact net operating income and long-term property values. It also provides sellers an organized, data-backed due-diligence report that highlights building performance and automates reporting and energy forecasting for investors.

Impact on Tenants

Retaining existing tenants is a challenge in the face of the threat posed by new, more energy- and water-efficient buildings. Tenants are attracted to these buildings, especially those who pay for their own energy and water consumption under a triple net lease. In response, developers are pursuing energy conservation certifications to show tenants they are providing them with long-term operational cost savings.

Building owners are addressing this challenge by including sustainability efforts up front in "green leases," which establish owner and tenant sustainability goals and responsibilities. However, clauses that cover noncompliance have yet to become standardized. It is also difficult to retrofit green features into existing leases or upon lease renewals, which increases the need for ongoing collaboration between tenants and owners to ensure tenant satisfaction and retention.

Impact on Investors

Investors are doing deeper due diligence to stay abreast of emerging and pending governmental sustainability regulation. This is especially true of new local municipal environmental requirements. In these areas, investors are looking for properties that have contingency plans that address the need to conform to, and mitigate the risk of, future environmental regulation. They are beginning to take a much harder look at the risks associated with sustainability, particularly the risk of obsolescence when sustainability measures are not adopted in light of changing tenant preferences, regulatory requirements and technology advancements.

Sustainability Summary

There is no doubt that CRE leaders will need to increase their knowledge of green building techniques that address sustainability. As the transition toward sustainability deepens, and the associated costs drop as technology improves, tenants will increasingly demand these improvements and be willing to pay the resulting rental premiums.

CRE needs to be proactive about energy management with a goal of increasing ROI through cost savings, increasing valuations by improving long-term property fundamentals, and by retaining good tenants and attracting environmentally conscious new ones. Owners of buildings with poor sustainability performance who fail to improve their properties will increasingly face a significant brown rental discount and eventual obsolescence.

Future demands for sustainability will come from multiple sources and will leave CRE with little option but to comply or suffer the loss as regulations and tenant demands force the issue.

Takeaway

Like its residential cousin, commercial real estate is an industry in flux. Outside investment, the rise of crowdfunding platforms, a deepening technology revolution, the proliferation of e-commerce, generational changes and the increasing popularity, and challenge, of sustainable design are ushering commercial real estate into a new era.

Realizing this, residential real estate leaders can take comfort in knowing they are not alone in facing a tsunami of change. They have to look no further than across the aisle at commercial real estate to dispel any doubts that the change forces they face are real and require their full attention, awareness and effort to create a prosperous future.

A Deeper Look
The key topics discussed in this chapter are adapted from the extensive examination of the state of commercial real estate today, presented in a report by T3 Sixty for the National Association of Realtors. That free, in-depth report, Commercial Real Estate ALERT, can be downloaded at nar.realtor/reports/commercial-real-estate-alert.

Navigate with Confidence

T3 Technology Solutions

- Tech Audits
- Digital Evaluations
- Product Strategy
- System Design
- RFP Development
- Project Management

T360

t360.com

08

Smart CRMs Go Mainstream

How Big Data and AI are Reinventing Relationship Management

A new generation of real estate customer relationship management systems are leveraging big data, machine learning and artificial intelligence to help brokers and agents convert contacts into clients, market to their farms and efficiently target prospects likely to transact. We call them Smart CRMs. A number of companies have cropped up in the last 24 months that either offer components of these new systems or serve as full-fledged Smart CRM platforms themselves. We take a deep dive into this budding trend and provide recommendations on how to best take advantage of it.

Smart CRMs

The rise of Smart CRMs accompanies developments in traditional CRM technology, consumer data, predictive analytics and artificial intelligence; Smart CRMs merge these into one platform designed to reduce the effort involved in cultivating and building consumer relationships and nurturing leads into clients. The integration of these technologies has created this new class of CRM, which will play a significant role in the way agents do business in the future and will eventually become the industry's de facto CRM technology.

Existing CRMs require enormous amounts of effort to operate, requiring diligence and constant management by agents who want to develop and maintain large databases of past and potential clients. Current real estate CRMs are essentially manually operated databases that enable agents to keep track of their contacts, perform bulk operations such as marketing, email and print, and operate their business in a repeatable, systematic way. This class of CRM remains useful, and aspects of this technology will be present in this new, emerging breed of CRM.

Smart CRMs apply predictive techniques to consumer data and behavior to surface contacts who are more important for agents to contact. Pattern-matching technology identifies the consumers most likely to transact and artificial intelligence technology suggests appropriate followup methods and messaging. Many Smart CRMs also serve as integration hubs that make it easier to ship consumer data to and from other tools agents use, which improves the recommendations Smart CRMs deliver. As they evolve, Smart CRMs are beginning to resemble a real estate agent personal assistant.

Start-up Funding

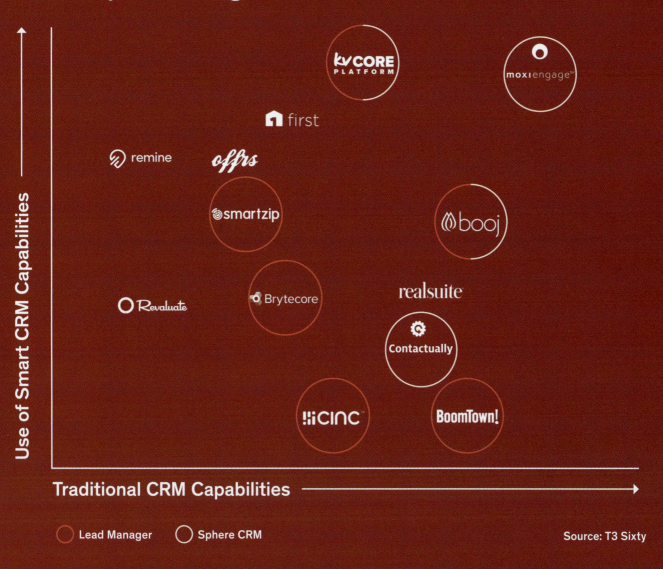

Big Data and Mining Contact Databases

Significant business and technology factors drive this development including a desire by brokers and agents to reduce transaction costs; brokers and franchisors' aspiration to generate business for their agents that circumvents the high costs of media and advertising; the new availability of personally identifiable data; advances in consumer-tracking technology; increased use of artificial intelligence and predictive analytics; and the rise of personalized marketing.

Elements of Smart CRMs

A lot of jargon is associated with technology, and Smart CRMs are no exception. Therefore, it is important to define some terms to help readers properly digest this chapter and better evaluate these technologies out in the field.

Behavioral Analytics
Behavioral analytics refers to the tracking and measurement of consumer behavior. In a Smart CRM context, this behavior is usually tied to specific users and used to evaluate their intent and interests. Tracked events can include opening emails, clicking on links in emails, interacting with websites, online advertisements, video and other online media. Tracked behaviors often include real estate-specific actions such as marking a property as a "favorite," saving a search and requesting information about a home. Behavioral analytics can be used to compare contacts or leads to assess their relative level of activity and interest. Most popular lead generation systems offer some degree of behavioral analytics to help agents sort more active prospects from both the thousands of leads these products can generate and the existing contacts in their databases.

Demographic Data
Demographic data covers consumer demographic information that allows a Smart CRM to potentially predict a consumer's likelihood of buying or selling. This information consists of life-stage events such as family status, age, income category and education level. This demographic information helps determine a consumer's likelihood of buying or selling.

Property-Based Data
Property-based data includes the data associated with a property and can include information such as the number of liens on a home, mortgage balance, time since the home was last bought or sold, estimated value of the home and estimated equity.

Financial Data
Financial data includes information about a consumer's financial life and can include credit scores or credit score ranges, wealth estimates and prospect financial behavior. It may include information related to purchasing and shopping behavior.

Lead Score
In most cases, lead scoring involves the use of behavioral analytics to score leads based on their perceived propensity to transact. Lead scoring can involve ranking contacts by their potential receptivity to contact and followup. Real estate lead scores have traditionally been built from prospect behavior, but as Smart CRMs have an increasing amount of data at their disposal, they are beginning to incorporate other demographic, property-based and financial data into their lead scores.

Propensity Score
A propensity score uses personally identifiable information to determine how likely a prospect is to transact. It is usually based on the demographic, property-based and financial information described in this chapter. Propensity scoring is used in many other industries, especially the financial services industry, to determine where marketing and prospecting efforts will be most effective. Real estate propensity scores often have a different terminology such as "Seller Scores" or "Buyer Scores" – denoting those who are more likely to sell or buy, respectively.

Relationship Score
Some Smart CRM tools coach agents on maintaining good relationships with contacts in their database by providing what is often called a "Relationship Score," which represents an agent's level of interaction with a certain prospect. Sometimes this is combined with other data to place more importance on maintaining contact with certain prospects (such as newly married couples, empty-nesters, etc.)

Automated Coaching
Many of the Smart CRMs on the market make use of either one or a combination of relationship, propensity, relationship or lead scoring to coach agents on who to contact in their database or lead-management system. Automated coaching software will often utilize the information learned from an agent's use of the system to suggest more effective actions. Some systems refer to automated coaching as "Recommended Actions."

Business Factors

In the past decade a significant amount of marketing dollars have been allocated to online media and lead generation companies. Agents and brokers are finding that these costs continue to rise over time. Online lead platforms such as Google, Facebook or other pay-per-click and pay-per-lead vendors operate as bid-oriented markets.

The bid model enables advertising platforms to collect as much as the market will bear. Over time, this has placed a significant premium on this customer acquisition strategy. Predictive analytics and Smart CRM technologies allow brokerages and agents to leverage the leads and contacts they already have. It also allows them to escape auction-oriented lead generation costs and increase their lead-conversion efficiency to maximize the investments they do make in lead generation. (For more on the online lead generation landscape, please see Trend No. 7, "The Big Four of Digital Real Estate.")

Brokers and franchisors have a growing interest in generating business for their agents without the high costs of media advertising or lead generation. As agents become increasingly independent and generate more business on their own, brokers struggle to defend their value proposition to agents. Smart CRMs offer one way for brokerages to provide their agents with significant value.

With Smart CRMs and predictive analytics technology, brokerages can significantly enhance agents' production without incurring the high costs of lead generation. Several technology vendors offer tools to brokerages and franchisors who can make it available to their agents.

> "The integration of these technologies has created this new class of CRM."

Technology Factors

Personally Identifiable Consumer Data

The availability of personally identifiable consumer data from a variety of sources plays a key role in the rise of Smart CRMs. In the past several years, data-industry vendors have packaged consumer information and made it more accessible to software developers. This information includes social media profiles, public records data, divorce filings, liens, property tax data, phone numbers and even financial data such as mortgage information and credit scores. Much of this data has been available for years, but the emergence of new ways to package, manage and share with software companies has changed. Through the use of application programming interfaces (APIs) and data-licensing, CRM software vendors are now able to access and build their own consumer information databases that augment their core CRM tool.

In just the last 24 months, new data companies have emerged that make consumers' personally identifiable browsing behavior available. This allows CRM companies to combine fundamental information about a consumer such as home address, credit score and mortgage balance with information about the websites they use, what and where they shop online, and other online behaviors that suggest they may be beginning to think about buying or selling a home.

The availability of all this consumer information has created a rich, new playground for CRM software companies to build smarter CRMs. In many cases, agents only need a tiny bit of information about a consumer, such as an email address or home address, to unlock a tremendous amount of information. Intimidating, powerful and definitely new territory for the industry!

Consumer-Tracking Technology

Consumer-tracking technology allows a software company to track everything consumers do on a website, and how they interact with emails, mobile apps and advertising. This technology is baked into many of the products agents currently use such as email-marketing systems, mobile apps and IDX websites. Agents can now monitor how consumers interact with their marketing and advertising. In addition, Smart CRMs use this behavioral information to score actions and gauge the transaction-readiness of specific contacts.

Predictive Analytics and Artificial Intelligence

The ability to combine behavioral and personal consumer data with predictive analytics and artificial intelligence techniques also drives the Smart CRM trend. When a large enough consumer database is paired with historical data showing which consumers ended up transacting, predictive software can reveal behavioral patterns and life situations that suggests consumers are more likely to purchase or sell a home.

Some of these techniques are simply extensions of common sense such as life events that typically trigger a home purchase or sale. Traditional indicators such as a new job, a new baby, death, divorce or other life events are obvious indicators. Less obvious triggers include changes in credit profile, wealth accumulation or demographic factors not as easily discernable. This data helps fine-tune predictive technology over time as algorithms verify which consumers with what data profiles end up transacting.

> "The use of data and personal information in consumer communications and marketing also fuels Smart CRM development."

Marketers already use this still relatively new technology to market products and services to consumers; it is only a matter of time before predictive analytics matures enough to predict consumers' real estate behavior to a high degree of accuracy.

Personal Marketing

The use of data and personal information in consumer communications and marketing also fuels Smart CRM development. Many agents currently send their entire database the same marketing; everyone gets the same newsletter, article or marketing piece. However, as consumer data makes its way into consumer marketing, brokers and agents will be able to take a more individualized approach to marketing.

For example, agents are less likely to send information about selling a home to a recent buyer; instead, they more likely want to send information about home improvements or tips on exploring the new neighborhood. Showing contacts something personally relevant is the key to effective consumer stay-in-touch programs and lifecycle marketing. Current industry stay-in-touch programs focus on homeownership and financial information relevant to homeowners. Expect this development to accelerate as software and marketing companies pursue more engagement from consumers through highly relevant messages and targeted information.

Smart CRMs in action

A number of companies are building Smart CRMs or provide tools that elevate existing CRMs into the Smart CRM category.

Some companies discussed below serve as data providers, focusing on the data or predictive analytics functions of Smart CRMs. In some cases, they are building, or intend to build, CRM platforms to make use of their data. In other cases, they focus on integrating with other CRMs to improve their capabilities.

While T3 Sixty interviewed these companies for this report, their inclusion is not an endorsement; they are used to illustrate the Smart CRM companies and technologies currently active in the industry. Look for future T3 Sixty case studies and reports for a deeper evaluation of specific Smart CRM products.

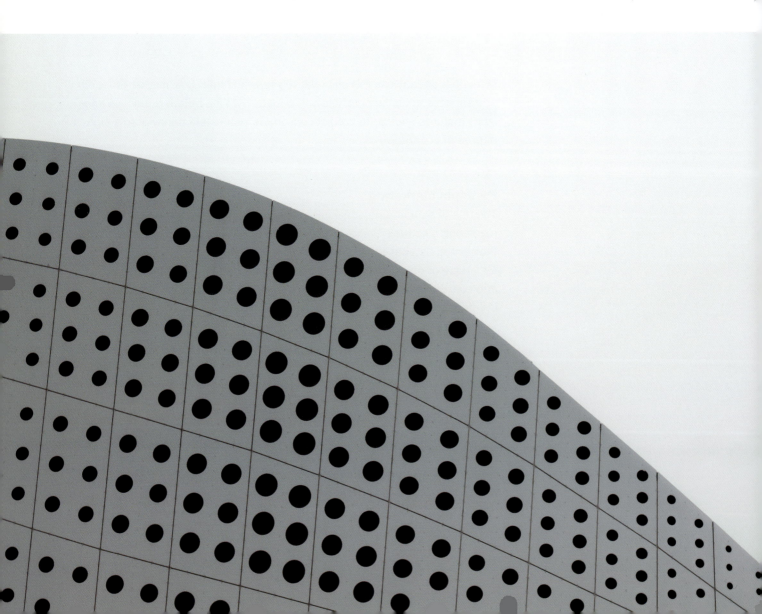

Companies Focused on Data or Predictive Capabilities

First

First (first.io) focuses primarily on helping agents convert leads in their existing databases. It uses social data including social connections, life-stage information and current residence data to identify opportunities in agents' databases. Agents import contacts into the First system to evaluate them.

The company currently offers three products. Audience Builder centralizes agents' contacts, deduplicates them and matches them to property data. Seller Scores applies First consumer data to contacts in agents' databases and scores them based on their likelihood of transacting. This product makes use of consumer data and predictive software to power the scoring. The third product, a mobile application called Conversations, suggests which contacts might be receptive to agent contact based on their Seller Score and their propensity for referring business. The application also displays the communication history with contacts to give agents a quick snapshot of their relationships.

First indicates that its mobile software monitors the outcomes of agent followup with contacts and uses the information to optimize the actions it suggests to agents. The firm is currently focused on selling directly to agents and teams and has integrated with two CRMs: Contactually (contactually.com) and LionDesk (liondesk.com).

Revaluate

Revaluate (revaluate.com) helps agents identify customers in their existing database or email system who are likely to move. Revaluate is not intended as a CRM platform, but rather a standalone contact-scoring system that works in conjunction with agents' existing tools.

The company's software integrates with third-party tools, agents' websites, public and private consumer data and tracks web search and spend activity to score prospects in an agent's database. Its product, Revaluate Pro, allows agents to either upload their databases into its system or to connect the system to their Google or Gmail account for automated synching.

The system then prompts agents to install a tracking script on their website and to activate integrations with third-party tools such as BombBomb (bombbomb.com), eEdge (kw.com/kw/eEdge.html), MailChimp (mailchimp.com), Mixmax (mixmax.com) and Placester (placester.com). These third-party integrations feed activity data back into Revaluate and are used to score prospects. The software then generates a weekly email that ranks the prospects in an agent's database based on their likeliness to move using Revaluate's "Move Score."

Revaluate is positioned as a tool dedicated to prospect scoring. Revaluate sells directly to agents and teams; it also has broker and enterprise pricing available for larger organizations. Revaluate has also developed a following in the mortgage and lending industries.

> "Smart CRMs apply predictive techniques to consumer data and behavior to surface contacts who are more important for agents to contact."

Remine

Remine (remine.com) bills itself as an intelligent property data system that annotates property data with mortgage, transaction and homeowner information. The company has positioned itself as a tool that helps agents more effectively focus their marketing and sales activities within neighborhoods they currently work or intend to farm. Remine has 100 percent coverage of public records data through a partnership with First American (firstam.com) and utilizes this data in conjunction with a database of hundreds of millions of U.S. adults.

Remine uses this data to rank the likelihood a consumer will transact or a property will hit the market. Remine uses maps as its primary interface; the platform is analogous to MLS and property tax data systems in look and feel. The maps make use of data visualization to quickly show where agents have opportunities to win business based on owner-occupancy, home equity and turnover rates.

Through MLS partnerships, Remine can display all transactions an agent has completed with their contacts; it also shows updated contact, property and other information for past clients, as well as the likelihood of a past client transacting again. Intended to supplement agents' existing CRM or through data export or API, Remine does not offer a standalone CRM. The tool is available only through MLSs as a core member benefit, while agents and brokers can purchase premium features. Like First, Remine currently has integrations with Contactually and LionDesk.

Brytecore

Brytecore (brytecore.com) scores leads and prospects in a system that integrates with other products or a broker or agent's website. The system uses a proprietary machine learning algorithm to score leads, segment them into groups such as "long-term prospect" and "immediate opportunity," and classify them into personas such as first-time homebuyers or move-up buyers.

Its system includes a CRM with lead-management and -routing capability and a mobile application for agents to use to respond to and manage leads. Brytecore is designed to be used by other technology companies or to enhance the lead-scoring, -management and -routing capabilities of a brokers' existing web platform. Atlanta brokerage Better Homes and Gardens Metro Brokers (metrobrokers.com) developed Brytecore before spinning it off as a separate company.

Companies Focused on Lead Generation

SmartZip

An early leader in predictive analytics, SmartZip (smartzip.com) offers a marketing platform that uses direct mail, digital advertising and prospecting tools to target marketing to homes and contacts likely to sell soon. Since introducing the predictive concept to real estate when it launched in 2009, SmartZip has added several products to its portfolio. Its original product, SmartTargeting, ranks the homes most likely to sell soon within a given area. More than one agent or brokerage can subscribe to each area. Subscribers can farm those homes through SmartZip's postcard farming system and through geo-targeted Facebook and Google advertising.

All postcards and online advertising direct consumers to landing pages that prompt them to contact the agent or broker sponsoring the area. The SmartTargeting product includes a lightweight CRM that enables subscribers to manage contacts with prospects. It includes two stay-in-touch tools: regular home value and market reports and direct mail followup.

The company recently added two additional products intended to help agents prioritize contact with prospects. Sphere applies predictive models similar to SmartTargeting to an agent's contacts, which subscribers can upload to the SmartZip system. Subscribers use the Sphere system to target likely sellers in their database and to generate referrals. SmartZip's newer product is an inside sales service that makes outbound prospecting and stay-in-touch calls to prospects that SmartZip identifies as most likely to transact. Prospects ready to talk to an agent are transferred to the SmartZip subscriber in that area. SmartZip offers its products to agents, teams, brokerages and larger organizations.

Offrs

Offrs (offrs.com) uses both predictive techniques and other services to verify consumer contact information and identify potential homesellers. The platform works for both targeted, territory-based marketing and prospecting and for surfacing promising prospects from agent databases. The company uses multichannel marketing to help clients engage prospects including online digital advertising, website landing pages, outbound phone calls and email homeowner surveys.

The company uses life-event data, property data and prospect behavioral activities to generate predictive scores. Offrs also conducts significant outbound data verification through phone calls and surveys to determine homeowners' interests in selling and the accuracy of their contact information. The ability for agents to follow up using social media and email are included in the platform. Intended to be used solely as a prospecting and lead-identification platform, Offrs does not include a CRM. The company sells its system through exclusive territory licenses and primarily focuses on sales to teams and agents.

Companies Focused on Smart CRM Capabilities

MoxiWorks

MoxiWorks (moxiworks.com) provides agents and brokerages a real estate platform that includes a suite of tools. The firm primarily focuses on medium-to-large brokerages and franchisors. Its tools include websites, presentation and CMA software, digital stay-in-touch programs, an intranet and a marketplace of third-party tools that integrate with the platform. Other features include a CRM, which the company recently enhanced with Smart CRM functionalities thanks to consumer data from public records, taxes, social media, shopping habits and education. The platform also accounts for changes in a household's makeup, including the arrival of children, recent divorces and new empty-nesters.

Financial information, including income, mortgage and investment history, and period of homeownership also help determine whether a consumer may be a potential seller or buyer. The system uses this data to provide agents insights on where consumers are in the homeownership journey and helps them more easily determine who in their database is most likely to make a move.

MoxiWorks fits best with brokerages who subscribe to a database-first education and coaching philosophy such as that advocated by popular coaching program Ninja Selling (ninjaselling.com).

KvCORE by Inside Real Estate

KvCORE is a real estate platform from Inside Real Estate (insiderealestate.com) that provides a web lead generation system, website and IDX search platform for agents and brokers. It includes a Smart CRM, integrates with transaction management systems and maintains a marketplace of applications that connect with the platform. The kvCORE Smart CRM tracks user behavior, including web, email, texting and social media to predict interests and to prioritize contact with leads. It also uses demographic and property-based data to develop propensity scoring. The Smart CRM provides coaching and recommends actions based on the data the system processes. The platform is sold primarily to brokerages and teams, and includes the popular Kunversion lead generation website platform.

RealSuite by realtor.com

Realtor.com unveiled a new, integrated lead-to-close CRM platform in 2017 called RealSuite (realsuite.io). Currently in beta testing, the platform is designed to streamline the agent and consumer experience throughout the real estate sales cycle, from prospect to close. The system uses behavioral analysis to suggest which contacts agents should reach out to and what messaging to use. RealSuite tracks consumer behavior to schedule automated followup actions such as emails and text messages on agents' behalf. RealSuite is sold directly to agents and teams.

> "Smart CRMs are beginning to resemble a real estate agent personal assistant."

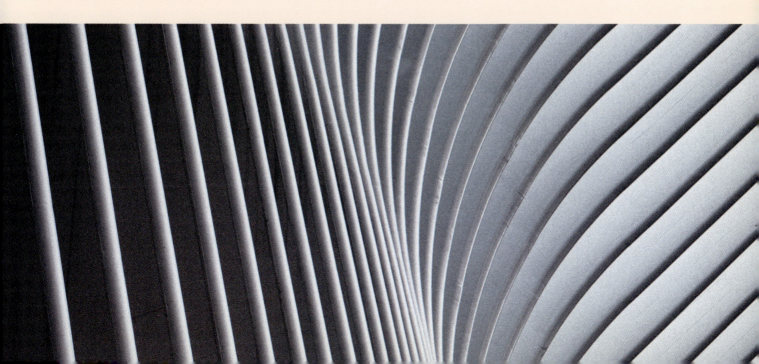

Companies Focused on Websites with Lead-Conversion Capabilities

BoomTown
BoomTown (boomtownroi.com) provides a full suite of services – CRM, lead generation, agent websites, predictive analytics and marketing followup tools. The CRM system is oriented around lead followup and uses predictive data to prioritize and suggest followup actions. Boomtown is sold primarily to teams and small brokerages who have a lead generation focus.

Commissions Inc.
Commissions Inc. (commissionsinc.com) is a lead generation product that includes a website, lead generation services, CRM and mobile apps. The system is primarily oriented toward lead followup and uses predictive scoring based on user behavior and user account activity. Commissions Inc. is sold primarily to teams and small brokerages with a lead generation focus. Fidelity National Financial (fnf.com) acquired the firm in 2016.

Takeaway

Real estate leaders looking at CRM and CRM-related products, including lead generation websites, broker websites and broker platforms, should not ignore Smart CRM technology as a selection criterion. Because this technology is becoming increasingly prevalent in off-the-shelf technologies available directly to agents, agents evaluating an organization's technology will likely consider CRMs without some level of Smart CRM technology out of date.

For organizations wanting to leverage the emerging Smart CRM trend in a tech purchase, consider the guidelines below for help determining what to focus on and the features to look for.

For organizations that already have a CRM platform, leaders should look for Smart CRM technologies designed to integrate with a brokerage or franchise CRM. The capabilities of these systems will likely include the annotation of contacts with data-borne information that helps brokers and agents prioritize or score contacts, validation tools that verify and de-duplicate contact information and suggestions for how to take action with contacts the system deems likely to transact soon. Some of these systems, such as BryteCore and Revaluate, include behavioral scoring that helps users identify contacts who become active, suggesting they may be likely to transact soon.

For organizations selecting CRM platforms for their company, leaders should look for technology providers that either include Smart CRM technology or provide synchronization to platforms that complement existing contact data with predictive technology. Company CRMs centered on working with an agent's sphere or contacts should focus on propensity scoring built from information about contacts (such as time in the home, soft credit score or life-event information). These systems should also ideally monitor contact relationships and suggest actions to improve them. Behavioral analytics is a nice addition if available, with agents receiving notifications if a contact becomes active on their website or starts opening or clicking on emails.

For organizations selecting lead generation technology, the inclusion of lead-scoring capabilities and suggested actions for contact are of utmost importance. When a lead generation strategy creates hundreds or even thousands of leads each month, it is critical that tools used by the organization can prioritize leads. Usually these solutions are based on user behavior, which is the minimum for this product category. More advanced products incorporate third-party data into their lead scoring, lead annotation and contact information verification.

Furthermore, organizations now have new options for lead generation that make use of consumer data available to personalized marketing that includes direct mail, digital advertising and targeted social media advertising. This flips the script on traditional lead generation; instead of waiting for a lead to come in and then score it, companies such as Offrs and SmartZip score the market, helping companies more effectively target potential customers.

The availability of consumer data and predictive technologies are rapidly becoming the norm in industry CRMs. Organizations seeking to implement CRM or lead generation technology in the next three years should strongly consider how to work Smart CRM technology into their strategies.

07

The Big Four of Digital Real Estate

The Real Estate Online Lead Generation Playbook

Real estate's digital revolution has revamped the way brokers and agents win and close business. Real estate brokerages and agents are spending an increasing percentage of their marketing dollars online. A significant portion of that digital spend goes to buying online leads from four platforms gaining ever more consumer mindshare and revenue dollars from brokers and agents: Facebook, Google, Zillow Group and realtor.com operator Move Inc. In this chapter, we take a step back and analyze the current paid lead generation landscape with a focus on these four predominant channels to provide brokerages and agents a comprehensive online lead gen playbook.

The Rise Of Digital Lead Generation

As the digital revolution increasingly bleeds deeper into all facets of life and business, the lead generation landscape has shifted dramatically, especially in real estate. With the rise of platforms such as Facebook, Google, Zillow and realtor.com, the way real estate agents and brokers communicate with prospects, how they run their businesses and how they generate leads differs widely from how their predecessors did a generation before.

Personal referrals buoyed by a high-profile local market presence have long anchored real estate agents' businesses. But the digital platforms discussed in this chapter have fundamentally altered how brokers and agents forge connections with prospects and clients. Whether it be Zillow and Trulia (owned by Zillow Group) and realtor.com with their tens of millions of monthly real estate visitors or Google and Facebook, who offer marketers big data-aided targeting advertising opportunities not available before, many brokers and agents rely on these digital middlemen to sustain and grow significant portions of their businesses.

Zillow Group consumer survey data shows 2017 was a turning point for online lead generation. In 2017, more homebuyers found their agent online (28 percent) than through a personal referral from a friend or relative (23 percent). Zillow Group's 2016 consumer survey showed that personal referrals still trumped online sources, 33 percent to 26 percent.

Real estate broker and agent ad spending tracks this trend. From 2011 to 2016, the annual amount brokers and agents spent on online ads relative to their overall ad spend nearly doubled from 48.2 percent to 84.9 percent, according to annual real estate ad spending reports from Borrell Associates Inc. (borrellassociates.com).

Real Estate Agent and Broker Ad Spending

Channel	2011 Estimated Spend (% of Total Spend)	2016 Estimated Spend (% of Total Spend)
Online	$6.5 Billion (48.2%)	$8.4 Billion (84.9%)
All Other Channels	$7.0 Billion	$1.5 Billion (15.1%)

Source: Borrell Associates Inc. Real Estate Advertising Outlook, 2013 and 2017

Marketing's Digital Transformation

Thirty years ago, marketers devised static messages to send to consumers that remained static for the duration of a campaign, which often ran for weeks. With the rise of digital, ads have become dynamic, with strategies and tactics evolving on a daily basis. Modern marketing must interact with real estate consumers where they are, and they are increasingly on Google, Facebook, Zillow, Trulia and realtor.com.

Digital marketers have metrics at their fingertips that would make their predecessors' heads spin. They get precise metrics around cost per lead, advertising reach, engagement, impressions and more.

Transformation of Marketing

Outreach
- **Then — Push marketing:** One-size-fits-all mass blasts using TV, radio, print
- **Now — Pull marketing:** Right message, right person, right time

Messaging
- **Then — Company products:** Communication focused on what the company offers
- **Now — Consumer needs:** Matching consumer needs and company products with empathy

Media Strategy
- **Then — Isolated channels:** Content consumed through siloed media channels
- **Now — Integrated channels:** Cohesive messaging across media moves buyers through their journey

Source: T3 Sixty

Borrell projects that online ads will account for 87.1 percent of the $10.5 billion brokers and agents will spend on advertising in 2017. Paid lead generation, of course, is just one part of what brokers and agents spend on ads, but if Zillow Group's sustained revenue growth serves as a reliable proxy, online lead gen is growing, too, by leaps and bounds. The tech giant saw a projected 26 percent annual revenue jump in 2017, following annual leaps of 31 percent and 98 percent in 2016 and 2015, respectively.

Unlike shoes, watches and other commoditized items, homes — and the agents who help sell them — present a unique, huge, emotional choice for consumers. The process of buying and selling homes is fraught with details, lots of money and regulation and a relatively long timeline, all of which add layers of complication to the online real estate lead-gen process for brokers and agents.

Paid Online Lead Generation

Marketing's digital revolution has shifted real estate's lead generation landscape. Brokers and agents still hunt down real estate consumers, but instead of predominantly reaching them through broad distribution channels such as newspapers, TV ads and offline advertising media, they either target them themselves through Google pay-per-click (PPC) advertising, through social media platforms or connect with them through real estate's predominant real estate portals Zillow, Trulia and realtor.com.

Instead of trusting intuition and using third-party data, digital lead generation allows marketers to measure almost every facet of the consumer journey, rigorously test campaigns and make fact-based decisions.

The rise of Zillow, Trulia and realtor.com has familiarized the industry with online leads. These portals predominantly deliver buyer leads from lead forms that consumers fill out on listing detail pages. Zillow Group, which owns Zillow and Trulia, and realtor.com, are also testing and developing seller lead products.

Of the 69 million consumers who visited real estate's 20 most popular sites in October 2017, nearly two-thirds visited Zillow, Trulia and realtor.com, according to data from the Hitwise division of Connexity.

Brokers and agents are also generating seller leads online. Campaigns tailored to sellers on Google and Facebook – notably the ubiquitous "What's My Home Worth?" ads – allow brokers and agents to target advertising to sellers and capture seller leads.

Most Popular Real Estate Sites

Rank	Site	Unique Vistors[1]
1	zillow.com	23.3 Million
2	realtor.com	11.5 Million
3	trulia.com	9.1 Million

Source: Hitwise division of Connexity
[1] Includes both desktop and mobile traffic, but not mobile app traffic.
Note on traffic numbers: These companies often report monthly unique visitors at much higher counts. There are several reasons for this including: a count that includes traffic to a network of sites; a unique visitor who visits from multiple devices, browsers and company mobile apps can be tallied as more than one visitor; and the lack of mobile app traffic included in the Hitwise methodology. While it does not include mobile app traffic, Hitwise's methodology accounts for unique visitors using multiple devices and browsers to access sites.

Online Lead Best Practices

- Develop a smart lead-process system that allows for quick responses and thorough followup.

- Ensure there is enough staff and team support to consistently follow the system.

- Respond to all leads as soon as possible, within at least five minutes.

- Track, optimize and improve.

- Gather context, such as search query and social media information, on each lead before calling; preferably, a system delivers this automatically.

- A call or in-person meeting is best; however, email, text messages and site-based chat are also viable options.

- Build rapport and get relevant information.

The Big 4 Of Real Estate Online Lead Generation

Online real estate lead generation is dominated by four companies: Facebook, Google, Zillow Group (which owns Zillow and Trulia) and Move Inc. (a subsidiary of global media company News Corp. and operator of realtor.com).

Each of these channels plays different roles in real estate's online lead generation landscape. Their differences range from the types of leads they deliver, advertisers' ability to target audiences and their costs and services.

Facebook and Google offer self-serve solutions, providing leads at higher points in the sales funnel; they require skillful handling and technology such as landing pages and CRMs that effectively incubate leads to facilitate cost-effective conversions. Zillow Group sites and realtor.com, on the other hand, provide hotter leads; these require speed, organization and streamlined procedures and skill for agents to close efficiently.

Company	2016 Revenue (YoY Growth)	2016 Net Income (Loss) (YoY Growth)
Facebook[1]	$27.6 Billion (54%)	$10.2 Billion (177%)
Google[1]	$90.3 Billion (20.4%)	$19.5 Billion (19.1%)
Zillow Group	$604 Million (35%)[2]	($200 Million) (-48.0%) [3]
Move Inc.	$108 Million (10%)	N/A[4]

Source: Public financial statements from Facebook, Google, Zillow Group and News Corp.
[1] Revenue from residential real estate advertising represents only a small part of these firms' overall revenue as presented.
[2] Agent advertiser revenue.
[3] Zillow Group's overall annual loss.
[4] News Corp., which acquired Move Inc. in 2014, does not break out Move's net income (loss).

Lead Funnel Characteristics of Real Estate's Most Popular Online Channels

Advertisers design campaigns to target specific audiences with ads on Facebook and Google. When consumers click on an ad, they are often taken to a landing page where the advertiser attempts to gather the visitor's contact information to turn them into leads.

Lead Generation Funnel

Popular Lead Source: Facebook leads typically enter at this stage.
Cost/Lead (aprx): $1-$15
Timing: Approximately two years from transaction

Top of Funnel (ToFu): Awareness

Clients are just beginning to think about buying or selling a home.

Popular Lead Source: Google leads typically enter at this stage.
Cost/Lead (aprx): $6-$10
Timing: Approximately one year before transaction

Middle of Funnel (MoFu): Research

Real estate clients begin online research about the value of their home if they are a seller or investigating neighborhoods and home prices if they are a buyer. They may reach out to agents for perspective at this stage

Popular Lead Source: Portal and agent/broker website leads typically enter at this stage.
Timing: Approximately 4 months before transaction

Bottom Of Funnel (BoFu): Active Search

Real estate buyers and sellers begin actively searching on real estate sites such as Zillow, Trulia and realtor.com. Consumers usually have an agent in mind at this stage.

Popular Lead Source: Broker/agent leads typically enter at this stage
Cost/Lead (aprx): $6-$10
Timing: Approximately 3-4 months before transaction

Selection

Real estate consumers interview agents and choose one that best meets their needs based on their research.

Transaction

Agent helps consumer transact. Agents should look to provide stellar service to win glowing reviews.

Post-Transaction

To increase the likelihood of repeat business and referrals, agents should keep in touch with clients with the help of a customer relationship management platform.

Source: T3 Sixty

Facebook and Google Online Lead Generation Chronology

1 Ad Engagement:
A Google or Facebook user sees a broker or agent's ad.

2 Landing Page:
The most effective landing pages align with the messaging and audience of the ad that generates the traffic.

3 Call-to-Action (CTA):
If the ad's call to action is strong enough and meets their needs, they will respond by clicking on it, which often takes them to a landing page on the advertiser's site.

4 Forms:
Advertisers strive to engage leads on landing pages with offers that will entice them to provide their contact information. That contact information initiates their life as a lead for that advertiser, with their information often automatically ported into a CRM.

5 Offers:
The offer that triggers the form-fill must be compelling and valuable enough to the user that they fill out the form. Common real estate offers include home price evaluations and homebuying guides.

On Zillow, Trulia and realtor.com, advertisers predominantly pay for leads off of the listing detail pages on those sites.

All four of these companies focus squarely on increasing their advertisers' return on investment by striving to deliver ever higher-quality leads and helping them convert leads at higher rates. Increased conversion rates lead to increased sales per delivered lead and increase what advertisers are willing to pay for the leads.

These companies can be slippery long-term partners as they can change models, revamp pricng, ad placement and more with a flip of the switch. Therefore, advertising success on the platforms requires constant vigilance, measurement and best practices refinement.

As online lead gen and these platforms mature, optimizing successful spends and strategies is becoming increasingly complicated. A host of agencies have emerged to help advertisers manage their campaigns as part of a technology spend or as a standalone service. Agencies charge advertisers from 10 to 30 percent of their total spend to manage these campaigns, with pricing varying by market and spend volume.

Optimized Online Real Estate Lead-to-Close Playbook

- **Online lead generation:**
  Facebook, Google, Zillow Group sites, and realtor.com are real estate's top paid online lead sources, according to T3 Sixty research.

- **Qualifying:**
  When they receive online leads, brokers and agents (or a service they hire) must quickly determine the leads' level of interest and transaction timeline, separate the casual browsers from the consumers ready to transact and determine where each lead is in the sales funnel. Some of the companies that offer qualifying services include: Zillow Concierge (exclusive to Zillow Group advertisers), Riley (getrileynow.com), Agentology (agentology.com), One Cavo (onecavo.com), Rokrbox (rokrbox.com), Boston Logic's Ace (ace.bostonlogic.com) and Phone Animal (phoneanimal.com).

- **Nurturing:**
  Not all leads are immediately ready to transact, which means brokers and agents must have a system to efficiently incubate them to maximize their online lead generation investments. Opcity (opcity.com) and Agentology are two services that do this on behalf of brokers and agents.

- **Strategic followup:**
  Brokers and agents can maximize their online lead generation spends by investing in CRMs and analytics tools that alert them to the contacts in their database who may be ready to transact based on changes in their digital behavior, such as an uptick in activity on a broker or agent's website, increased responses to drip emails and other big data triggers. Predictive analytics firms First (first.io) and Revaluate (revaluate.com) and CRMs such as Follow Up Boss (followupboss.com), Chime (chime.me) and Contactually (contactually.com) do this. For more on this class of emerging tools see Trend No. 5 "Smart CRMs Go Mainstream."

- **Closing the client:**
  Agents present services and generate trust to convert the lead into a client.

- **Transaction:**
  Agents provide excellent services, planting seeds for receiving a good rating and review from their clients.

- **Post-transaction:**
  Agents secure ratings and reviews. Platforms that help brokers secure feedback from clients include RealSatisfied (realsatisfied.com) and Reach150 (reach150.com).

- **Followup:**
  Agents use systems to keep in touch with clients to facilitate repeat business and referrals. Most real estate CRMs have tools to help brokers and agents efficiently follow up with drip emails and provide reminders of significant dates and other events.

Based on T3 Sixty's interviews and research, the cost per qualified lead – with "qualified leads" defined as those who are ready to speak or meet with a real estate agent – for each of the four channels currently converges at approximately $120 when paired with a refined lead-qualification process. However, the strategy and pathway from ad to contact to appointment differs for each channel, as does cost, which is dictated by advertising strategy, a market's marketing demand and home prices. The latter determines commission amounts and, thus, what agents are willing and able to pay for leads.

Facebook

Overview
Over 1.3 billion people around the world use Facebook on a daily basis. It has become an intimate and integral part of most consumers' lives, especially in the U.S. The platform now has over 5 million advertisers and raises its ad prices as demand increases.

Snapshot

Ads Overview	Users have access to a detailed, comprehensive self-serve back-end ad manager that allows them to choose campaigns with a variety of goals, formats, target audiences and more. Users can also create easy ads by "boosting" posts on their Facebook Business pages.
Lead Profile	Top of funnel. Because most consumers use Facebook to catch up with friends and news, leads generated on the platform tend to be further away from a transaction than other channels discussed in this chapter. Successful conversion requires a smart, consistent incubation strategy.
Pricing	Varies by type of campaign and ad quality; costs per lead typically range from $1 to $15.

One of Facebook's hallmarks as an advertising platform is its targeting capability. Advertisers tap into the platform's vast information about specific users to target those they believe will be most responsive to their ads, products and services. Facebook is constantly iterating on targeting. One of its innovative targeting mechanisms is Lookalike Audiences, a tool unveiled five years ago that allows advertisers to target ads to audiences that "look like" a set of contacts they upload or specify. Facebook uses a machine learning algorithm to optimize the Lookalike Audience.

The company is increasingly focusing on delivering results that directly meet advertisers' business goals, such as sales rather than proxy metrics such as visits, engagements and clicks.

How it works
The simplest Facebook ads involve paying to advertise organic posts; advertisers publish a post on their company's Facebook Business timeline and then click "Boost Post." They choose an objective – traffic to their website or engagement on Facebook – target audience demographic, location, interests and behaviors, and set their total budget and duration and then click "Boost."

Advertising gets much more sophisticated with Facebook's Ads Manager dashboard, which gives advertisers the ability to build more detailed, nuanced campaigns. Advertisers choose from a variety of ad formats including photo, video and photo montages and then determine where the ads show up, whether in the newsfeed or right rail (on desktop), mobile newsfeed, or let Facebook choose a mix. By adding a piece of Facebook-provided code to their website (known as a Facebook Pixel), advertisers can track conversions, see Facebook-derived audience behavior on their sites and track visitors for retargeting campaigns. As with Boosted Posts, they can hone their audience by location, demographics (age, gender), interests and behaviors.

Facebook uses artificial intelligence and its vast amounts of consumer data to hone its algorithms to help advertisers more effectively target prospects. For example, real estate advertisers can target those users the platform suggests are "Likely to move" based on data from Facebook and property tax, assessor and deed information from third-party marketing data company Epsilon.

"Real estate Facebook advertising has clearly gone mainstream."

Advertisers can also choose to direct ads to custom audiences, which include known contacts (those in contact databases, website visitors and app users) and Lookalike Audiences, which leverages Facebook's algorithms to create audiences similar to a set of customers, contacts and website visitors that advertisers specify.

In 2017, Facebook rolled out a real estate-specific ad product for brokerages and real estate agent teams with at least 100 listings, Dynamic Ads for Real Estate. To participate, brokerages and agent teams must integrate their listing data and search systems with Facebook's ad platform. Facebook monitors the listings consumers visit on the brokerage advertiser's site and then displays the same or similar listings from the broker on Facebook or Instagram in a slideshow format.

Lead Profile

Facebook leads reflect how consumers use the platform. Consumers typically do not go to Facebook to find answers to real estate questions, look for agents or listings. Instead, they use the network to keep up with news from their friends and family and the brands and businesses they follow. This makes Facebook a good branding opportunity for brokers and agents, but, aside from the new Dynamic Ads for Real Estate product, not for driving leads with short conversion timelines.

Facebook leads are typically earlier in the buying process and require a smart, diligent followup process and a longer timeline to close. Given their location higher up the funnel, these leads are also less expensive than those from Google, Zillow Group sites and realtor.com. While Facebook gives advertisers the ability to easily and relatively cheaply initiate conversations with prospects and to highly target their advertising, the platform delivers a high prevalence of leads and prospects many months or years out from transacting.

Pricing

Facebook ads are becoming more popular, and expensive. The price per ad more than quadrupled from 2014 to 2016 and is expected to increase significantly. Like Google and Zillow Group ads, Facebook ad prices are based on an automated auction format with higher-demand audiences costing more and lower-demand audiences less. Depending on campaign type, advertisers pay by impression or action, such as PPC.

Prices differ by audience, market and season with the cost of each Facebook lead ranging from $1 to $15, according to T3 Sixty research. The cost per qualified lead – those ready to speak or meet with a real estate agent – is much higher, approximately $120 per lead.

Winning Strategies

Successful Facebook advertising starts with segmenting audiences and tailoring ads to match each one. Branding ads work best when targeting a large audience, when advertisers simply want to broadcast the existence of their service to consumers. For the consumers who have interacted with the brand – which advertisers know by the metrics Facebook provides – advertisers can deliver ads tailored toward building trust. For those whose behavior indicates they are further down the sales funnel, advertisers can deliver ads designed to drive appointments.

The Facebook marketing firm Curaytor (curaytor.com) recommends agents focus on boosting posts rather than diving into Ads Manager. While advertisers may sacrifice between 10 to 15 percent ROI by going with the simpler Facebook ad program, they often save time that they can use to hone their messaging and ads to better engage their target audience.

Because Facebook audiences are so much higher in the real estate sales funnel than other online lead sources, retargeting is a powerful tool for advertisers to use. By using a Facebook Pixel on their website, brokers and agents can target ads to consumers who visit their site. Advertisers can also upload specific contacts to target on Facebook or across the third-party websites and apps in Facebook's ad network.

Facebook advertisers also find success by building campaigns that include a blend of targeting and retargeting. First, they run a campaign to entice consumers to click an ad and then target subsequent ads designed to increase brand awareness to that audience.

> "The paid online lead generation landscape has never been more dynamic."

Real estate marketers have found success with Facebook Lead Ads, one of the platform's newer campaign objectives. Lead Ads are designed to collect prospect email addresses and other information advertisers want directly within Facebook – no external landing page needed. Facebook pre-populates the forms with prospect information it already has, lowering the barrier to entry on successful submissions and increasing the percentage of accurate contact information advertisers receive. Advertisers can automatically input these leads directly into their CRM or input them manually.

Other Facebook advertising best practices:

- Facebook ads should have at least one high-quality, engaging photo, if not a video. The latter is especially effective for agents who are engaging on camera.

- Ads should feature an engaging call to action to spur interest. For example, agents can post photos of an attractive listing and leave off price and address to arouse curiosity.

- Landing pages should align with ad and audience.

- Followup sales scripts should align with the ads that triggered the lead.
- Sales strategies should start out soft as many Facebook leads are further away from transacting.
- Refresh ads at least monthly. This prevents campaigns from going stale and from consumers seeing the same ad too many times.
- Create multiple ads for each campaign to test and increase effectiveness – Facebook will automatically surface a campaign's best-performing ads.
- Optimize ads for specific website actions such as visiting an "About Us" page or conducting a search. Advertisers can track these with a Facebook Pixel and specify them in Ad Manager.
- Utilize Lookalike Audiences and refine targeting with third-party data.

Google

Overview

Google offers a variety of ad products, but its PPC product, AdWords (google.com/adwords), is its most popular. AdWords advertisers bid for keywords and phrases that match queries consumers make on the Google search engine; AdWords users can also direct ads to YouTube video ads and display ads, but this chapter focuses on the most popular in real estate: search engine ads. The text-only search ads show up at the top and bottom of Google's search results pages, on both mobile and desktop devices. Advertisers can target audiences by location, language and device type.

Snapshot

Ads Overview	With Google's most popular ad product, AdWords, advertisers place text-only ads on Google search results pages for specific keyword search terms. They bid on having their ads appear on the search results pages for those keywords.
Lead Profile	Middle of the funnel. Google leads have demonstrated intent by clicking on an ad, so they tend to require less effort to convert into clients than Facebook leads but more effort than portal leads.
Pricing	Google leads are often more expensive than Facebook leads with estimated cost per lead ranging from approximately $6 and $10 based on T3 Sixty research. Prices can vary widely based on market and the demand for the keywords advertisers target.

AdWords advertising is all about intent. Consumers demonstrate their potential interest in a product or service by conducting a Google search. Advertisers piggyback on that intent by advertising their services in the organic search results that Google presents to consumers (Google uses artificial intelligence and machine learning to filter results in an algorithm it calls RankBrain). Optimizing for placement in Google's organic search results – known as search engine optimization (SEO) – involves a different strategy than paid lead generation, known as search engine marketing (SEM).

How It Works
Google uses consumers' search activity to determine their interest in a topic. In this way, Google aims to deliver the right message to the right audience at the right time. AdWords ads show up on Google search results pages above and below organic search results (up to four ads in each location). By default, ads also show up across Google's Display Network, which includes third-party websites that have signed up to host Google ads. Advertisers can choose to have their ads only show up on Google-powered search results pages.

Like Facebook, Google AdWords offers advertisers a comprehensive self-serve backend platform to design, target and buy ads. Advertisers pick keywords that align with the consumer Google queries that their product or service is built to solve or answer. Advertisers can determine the relative popularity of specific keywords and their search volumes using Google's Keyword Planner, which also suggests the amount advertisers should bid to win placement. AdWords users can target ads to consumers in specific locations, by search language and the device type they use; they can also target users who have previously visited their website with remarketing campaigns.

Advertisers set a daily budget for their campaign and a bid amount for their keywords, which advertisers can direct Google to automatically set or they can set it manually. Google determines pricing through its auction pricing algorithm when ads run. The more popular targeted keywords cost more, less popular keywords are cheaper. Google chooses to display ads based on whether an advertiser has a winning bid and the platform's determination of an ad's "quality," determined by click-through rate, ad relevance and landing page experience.

AdWords ads feature a landing page link, two headlines (up to 30 characters each) and a description (up to 80 characters). Google makes certain ads available for Ad Extensions that allow advertisers to add specific site links, phone numbers, office locations and more to their ad. Google's Ad Rank algorithm determines whether or not an ad is eligible for Ad Extensions.

Lead Profile
Google leads are further down the purchase funnel than Facebook leads. They expressed active interest in an advertised product or service by clicking

> "Instead of trusting intuition and using third-party data, digital lead generation allows marketers to measure almost every facet of the consumer journey."

the ad, so a higher proportion are typically warmer than Facebook leads. They are actively searching for a solution to their challenge or answer to their question, and clicked on an ad for a service they think may solve or answer it.

As with many Facebook ads (aside from the Facebook Lead Ads discussed above), Google AdWords leads hit an advertiser's landing page. How the landing page aligns with the ad, the clarity and appeal of its design, its load time and the effectiveness of its calls to action influence how successful an AdWords campaign is in converting the website traffic it delivers into genuine leads who provide their contact info for followup.

Because advertisers can target ads to property niches and specific neighborhoods through keywords, they can generate highly targeted leads. In some cases, advertisers can also see leads' Google search queries, which helps facilitate richer conversations and increases conversions. However, Google leads can be plagued by a high prevalence of inaccurate contact information. Approximately a quarter of registrations from Google can have false contact information, according to T3 Sixty research. That percentage can vary by ad-targeting skill, market and landing page quality.

Pricing

AdWords prices vary widely based on the keywords advertisers target. Long-tail keywords — those that include more words or specificity — can go for a few cents-per-click, while more popular keywords, such as the name of a high-demand, luxury neighborhood, can be many dollars-per-click. However, price does not necessarily correlate to a keyword's ability to drive conversions or ROI. Sometimes cheaper long-tail phrases reach fewer people but have higher conversion rates.

Winning Strategies

AdWords success centers on making ads relevant to the keywords advertisers target. If ads do not align with the keywords they show up with, consumers will be less likely to click on the ads and Google will charge more for placement.

To achieve efficiency, advertisers must segment their audiences and ads properly and align ads and audiences with campaign-specific landing pages. If an ad promises insight on Beverly Hills real estate, the landing page consumers reach when they click on the ad should provide insights on Beverly Hills real estate. A disconnect will drastically lower conversion rates.

Other AdWords best practices:

- Tune into how consumers search. Advertisers should put themselves in their prospects' shoes and conduct market research to uncover promising keywords. A little creativity and research can help marketers reach valuable audiences with lower-cost, better-performing keywords and key phrases.

- Conduct a search analysis. Advertisers should research how consumers arrive at their site, and choose related keywords. They can also perform this research with the help of third-party applications like Moz ([moz.com](moz.com)), SEMRush (semrush.com) and Keyword Tool (keywordtool.io).

- A good rule of thumb for advertisers new to AdWords is to focus campaigns on the neighborhoods within 10 miles of their farm.

- Advertisers should claim their business on Google Maps, which ensures that it will appear in Google Maps search results.

- Advertisers should also participate in Google's ratings and reviews program, which surfaces the Google ratings and reviews when consumers search for their business on Google.

Portals

Snapshot

Ads Overview	Zillow Group sites (Zillow and Trulia) and Move Inc.'s realtor.com primarily deliver leads to advertisers through contact forms on listing detail pages. Though they operate differently, these portals deliver similar kinds of leads at comparable prices, according to T3 Sixty's research.
Lead Profile	Generally, bottom of the funnel. Leads are relatively high-quality and convert at higher rates. Because these leads are actively searching and contacting agents on real estate sites, agents must act quickly to capture them as clients as they are likely reaching out to more than one broker or agent.
Pricing	Most expensive of the channels analyzed in this chapter. The costs per lead stand at approximately $120 as buyers are near the bottom of the sales funnel, ready to transact.

Zillow Group

Overview

Zillow Group, which owns Zillow and Trulia, sent its agent advertisers (aka "Premier Agents") nearly 17 million leads in 2016. Over 84,000 agent advertisers were paying the firm an average of $632 per month for leads at the end of 2016.

Zillow Group's bread and butter agent ad product — Premier Agent Ads — places the contact information, photo, Zillow profile rating and review count of up to three agent advertisers on for-sale listings across its family of consumer sites (Zillow, Trulia, RealEstate.com, StreetEasy, HotPads and Naked Apartments). The company charges advertisers for the ad impressions it delivers on a ZIP code-basis (listing agents are automatically included on listing detail pages). Agents receive a lead when consumers fill out a contact form and click a checkbox next to their name.

Premier Agents can purchase two optional add-on products: Seller Boost and Premier Agent Direct. For Seller Boost, Zillow Group connects agents with leads from contacts on detail pages of homes not for sale; these include home price requests from an owner dashboard Zillow Group offers homeowners. Premier Agent Direct increases agents' branding by promoting agent advertisers' listings on Zillow, Trulia and Facebook.

The company is also testing seller leads through the controversial Zillow Instant Offers product, which the portal began testing in two markets in mid-2017. Instant Offers connects homesellers with investors who provide offers on their homes. Zillow Group encourages these homeowners to request a price estimate from a local agent to evaluate the bids better. It expanded the test to Phoenix in August 2017 with two broker partners who receive the listing leads the program generates. See Trend No. 2, "Enter the Direct Buyer," for a detailed analysis of this trend.

Zillow Group also has a broker-focused ad product — Premier Broker — that allows brokers to buy ads under their brand and route leads to their agents.

Zillow Group is focused on increasing the conversion rates of the leads it delivers to agents. In 2015, it introduced a lead-scrubbing service — Zillow Concierge — to quickly respond to and qualify leads on advertisers' behalf. Concierge, and its hundreds of employees helping scrub leads, is intertwined with the Premier Agent and Broker program. It is available to a subset of its advertisers, at no additional cost, and the company is working to scale up the service to support more advertisers. Business interests drive this move; Zillow Group's executives talk about improving advertisers' conversion rates and ROI with the expectation that those increases will drive ad prices higher (Zillow Group uses an auction-based pricing system for ads, so, for the most part, price increases follow supply-demand economics).

In fall 2017, Zillow Group dove deeper into improving advertisers' lead generation with the introduction of a service that helps broker advertisers devise best practices and hold agents accountable. Zillow Group "Performance Consultants" serve as brokers' lead-conversion coaches.

Agent and team profiles play a huge role in the Zillow Group lead generation platform. The company began presenting unfiltered consumer ratings and reviews in 2010 on agent profiles and automatically began adding transaction histories to them in 2013. It recently updated the profile design to better accommodate agents on teams. Consumer ratings on a five-star scale and the total number of an agent's Zillow reviews appear next to a head shot in Premier Agent ads on listing detail pages.

> "It's impossible to overstate the way marketing has changed."

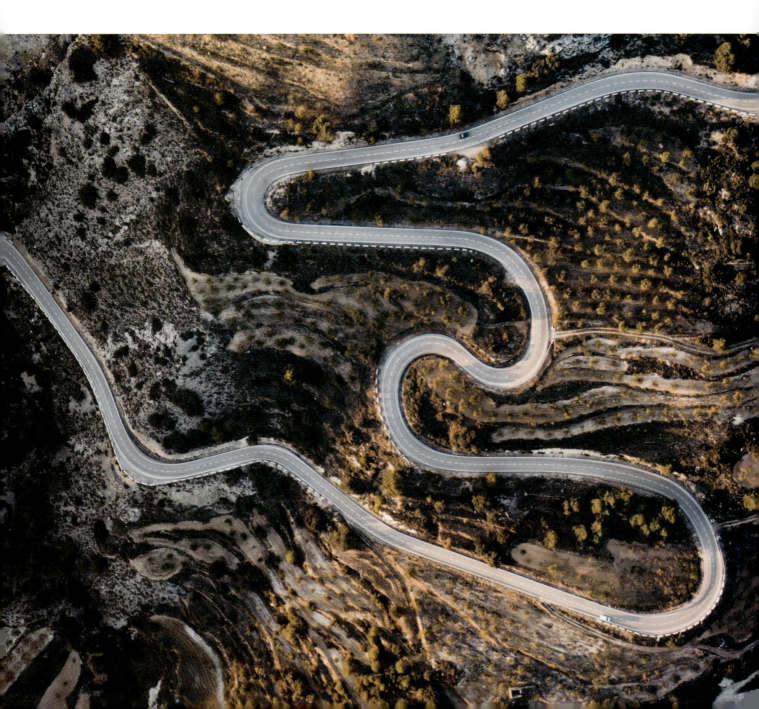

Realtor.com

Global media giant News Corp. – owner of The Wall Street Journal, Barron's, HarperCollins Publishers and Australia-based real estate portal REA Group Limited – acquired realtor.com operator Move Inc. in late 2014. Since then, realtor.com's relatively new parent company has revamped the brand, grown its traffic and redesigned its platform, but the core advertising product remains the same.

Like Zillow Group, realtor.com's central ad product centers on selling consumer contacts generated by contact forms on the site's listing detail pages to agents and brokers under the Connections for Buyers product name. Unlike Zillow Group, these contact forms do not include any agent advertiser details; they are unbranded contact forms. Advertisers purchase this sub-

> "The paid online lead generation landscape has never been more dynamic."

scription ad product on a ZIP code basis. It is available in two forms: Flex, where just one advertiser receives the lead, and Fast, where two advertisers receive the lead at the same time.

Realtor.com offers Advantage Pro, which allows brokerages and agents to pay more for the right to exclusively receive all of the leads on their realtor.com listings and choose how to distribute them; the firm offers the product on an all-or-nothing basis. The company also offers a pure branding ad package, which places display ads for brokers and agents on realtor.com search results pages. The portal is beta-testing a seller-leads product it launched in fall 2017 that delivers leads to agents from a homeowner dashboard called My Home.

Realtor.com revamped its agent profiles in 2015 to include unfiltered ratings and reviews and MLS-sourced transaction histories. As with Zillow Group ads, fleshed-out profiles on realtor.com help agents with lead conversion. When consumers receive a contact from an agent advertiser they often do research on them. Both realtor.com and Zillow Group agent profiles show up high in organic search engine results for agents' names.

Portal Best Practices
As consistently the hottest leads in the online real estate lead generation landscape, portal leads require speed. These buyers and sellers are ready to engage around real estate and have reached out to an agent for help; if an agent (or someone on the agent's behalf) does not respond soon, they will

move on to someone else — many agents are eager to speak to a hot lead. This requires having the technology, systems and team in place to ensure that agents maximize their portal spends. Without this organization, they will see lower returns on their portal investments and potentially be priced out as competitors convert at higher clips and thus can bid more for the leads.

Have a smart lead-incubation strategy. Portal leads might need a bit of nurturing before they are ready to sign on the dotted line. Smart CRMs, and the big data insights and automation they provide, are becoming critical tools in this realm. For more on Smart CRMs, see Trend No. 8, "Smart CRMs Go Mainstream."

Takeaway

The digital revolution has fundamentally changed the way real estate marketing works. Advertisers no longer devise static campaigns that run relatively untouched for months. Modern real estate business generation is a daily, metric-heavy affair, requiring deep knowledge, organized processes and a clear understanding of the entire landscape.

As the digital era deepens, more real estate consumers visit, and trust, the online platforms covered in this chapter: Facebook, Google, Zillow, Trulia and realtor.com. As such, real estate professionals need to develop smart, polished processes for generating business from them.

Facebook's focused jump into real estate with its Dynamic Ads for Real Estate product that it launched in summer 2017 provides a clear affirmation that brokers and agents need to develop and sharpen their online lead gen strategies. The continued evolution of the other popular real estate lead gen channels – Google and the large portals – requires that brokers and agents begin implementing campaigns on each platform that maximize the strengths and minimize the weaknesses of each.

Attracting leads is one thing; equally important is having the systems and tools in place to convert them efficiently and effectively. As competitors become more efficient, prices for these leads will increase, pricing out those who do not jump on and master the online lead-gen arts.

Enabling Smart Change

T3 MLS + Association

- Meeting Facilitations
- Mergers + Consolidations
- Market Assessments
- Transaction Options
- Governance + Ownership
- Technology Selection
- Transaction Planning
- MLS Innovation

t3mls.com
t360.com

06

Design as a Service

A Brokerage Playbook to Support Strong Agent Brands

For decades, real estate agent marketing has suffered from dated designs, generic layouts, headshots and messaging focused on an agent's services, not the consumer's needs. However, real estate marketing is improving as some newer brokerages are using high-quality design and branding to help their agents stand out from the competition. Consumer-centric, emotionally relevant and innovative, these firms invest in helping their agents stand out from the crowd. We provide a playbook here for you to do the same.

Design as a Service

Brokerages are beginning to extend a more sophisticated marketing mindset to their agents by offering them customized marketing services. While this provides agents greater support and higher quality marketing, the broker's entire brand benefits. As a result, some brokerages are achieving significant success and beginning to pioneer a new kind of brokerage. But offering customized marketing services to agents that makes business sense and gets results requires vision, investment and a refined process.

Through the end of the 20th century, well-designed marketing materials were limited to brokers and agents who could afford skilled designers. Over the past few years, the internet has helped the gig economy blossom, and, as a result, real estate brokers and their agents have gained access to qualified marketing professionals around the world. This has allowed even the smallest real estate brokers and agents at various production levels to afford attractive brand designs.

Millennials grew up with this high standard of design, and as they entered the workplace they came to expect it from their brokerage and their personal branding. This expectation contrasts with the traditional real estate brokerage model, which features a lean staff that provides a basic operational platform to agents. While this approach allows agents to be "the CEO of their own desk," offering flexibility and control over their professional lives, agents are left to fend for themselves to create their own marketing materials, write their own presentations and manage their own transactions.

When agents focus on growing their business, these operational requirements can be burdensome and distracting. And when agents build their own brands, the broker's brand can splinter from inconsistent quality and a variety of styles and messages. These are some of the reasons why some brokerages are beginning to leverage design as a service and why more should consider doing so.

> "This has allowed even the smallest real estate brokers and agents at various production levels to afford attractive brand designs."

The Service-Centric Model

Many brokerages have met the needs of the modern workforce by going beyond the traditional brokerage model and instituting a service-centric model. Rather than leaving agents to manage the details of their own business, the company provides additional support, often in the form of transaction management and marketing staff. This strategy delivers a range of benefits, from providing a cohesive and minimum level of service for all agents to having a marketing team dedicated to actively maintaining every facet of the consumer experience. However, the brokerage needs to pay for the staff through splits and administration fees.

Even brokerages with this model find there is a gap between agent need and company services: Agents who would like to create a personalized, custom brand – one that is specific to them – still must manage the process themselves under this setup. Creating a personal brand can be an expensive and time-consuming task as it includes selecting a designer, setting design objectives and keeping projects focused on the end goal. Most brokerages are not set up to service the needs of individual agents at scale.

Some brokerages have addressed this challenge by taking the service-centric brokerage model one step further by building the infrastructure to help agents create dynamic brands at scale. They have hired a team of marketing professionals who create and manage custom design services for individual agents. Effectively, the brokerage runs its own design firm with its agents as its primary clients.

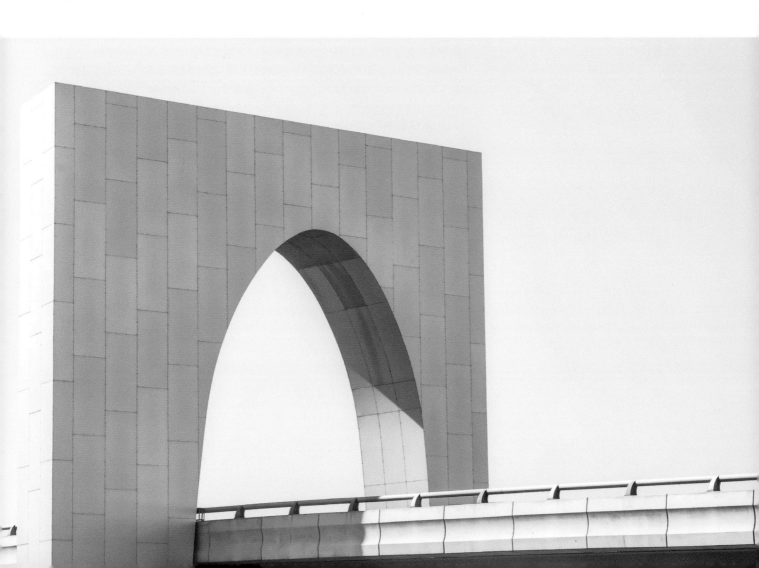

In this environment, marketing staff goes beyond managing the broker's brand; they provide a complete range of marketing support for individual agents. This could include the creation of agent logos, brand systems, branded templates for property flyers and postcards and fully customized property brochures. It may also include the services of specialists in digital and print marketing, party planning, social media, content creation, data analysis and public relations.

Furthermore, some brokerages offer in-house printing services that provide custom, hardbound presentations and property signage, for which they can charge below-market rates while providing short turnaround times. It is difficult to compete against this combination of marketing quality, speed and low price.

This approach to marketing services is not new, however. Companies such as Halstead (halstead.com) in the New York area and @properties (atproperties.com) in Chicagoland have experienced success with this strategy for well over a decade. Brokerages that currently employ this model are ones that can afford to offer an increased level of service, particularly those which focus on the luxury market in major metropolitan areas.

Leaders who are innovative, visionary and able to overcome the startup cost of these services receive a wide range of benefits, including recruiting, retention and brand differentiation. Brokerages such as M Realty (mportlandhomes.com) in Portland, Oregon; PorchLight Real Estate Group (tgroup.com) and Urban Luxe (urbanluxerealestate.com) in Denver; @properties; The Agency (theagencyre.com) in Los Angeles; and Compass (compass.com) in 11 large U.S. metros are leading the way with this strategy.

The Agency Creates

Founded in 2011, The Agency manages offices across North America but is primarily based in the greater Los Angeles area. It has 180 agents that generate over $4 billion in sales volume by focusing on the ultra-luxury category.

Its marketing division, The Agency Creates (theagencycreates.com, TAC), takes a unique approach to its marketing services. Not only does it offer marketing to clients outside of real estate, it is profitable.

Launching The Agency brand cost over $150,000, but after six months the firm had little to show for its efforts. This did not deter the leadership; high-quality and innovative marketing was part of the company's DNA. "Most of our competitors don't have the same tolerance for pain," says Mike Leipart, managing partner of TAC.

The owners continued to hire marketing staff and create content on a daily basis. Within two years the department was profitable, and the company website attracts approximately 2 million unique visitors per year.

TAC employs 30 full-time staff to support the brokerage's 180 agents. This is a ratio of one staff member for every six agents, the lowest ratio in T3 Sixty's analysis.

Reasons to Consider

Brokerages benefit in multiple ways by offering custom marketing services. It helps them with agent recruitment and retention, win listings for their agents, and increase the power and reach of both their brand and those of their agents. These benefits are expanded on below.

Recruitment and Retention

The greatest advantage of adopting custom design services applies to a broker's ability to recruit and retain agents. New recruits rarely have access to this level of service; merely walking them through the marketing department and presenting examples of past work can be impressive and impactful. Agents who currently work with the brokerage are less likely to leave because they actually use this higher level of support generally not found at other brokerages.

Get the Listing

In ultra-luxury markets where listings are often priced above $10 million, agents are in fierce competition. In listing presentations, they will present top-notch marketing materials. By creating custom marketing materials specific to the style and message of the listing, agents can stand apart from the competition, exceed the owner's expectations and win more of these coveted listings.

However, Leipart believes this level of support is not scalable, nor should it be. The Agency's goal is not to be the biggest, but the best, and it could not offer the same high level of quality if it had 1,000 agents. The extremely high sales prices of the homes its agents help sell allows the firm to afford this luxury version of design as a service.

Leipart believes that a commitment to not using freelancers contributes to the department's success. "Outside firms have boundaries around process and timelines," he says. "They're not focused on protecting our business. Staff will stay up late to get things done."

TAC offers creative services to its agents at cost, which is significantly less than what they would pay another vendor. As a result, the department handles almost 100 percent of agents' custom marketing projects. Profitability comes from its external clients, which are primarily new developments. It does not actively sell services to non-real estate clients such as restaurants and dance companies, but offer them on a case-by-case basis when a good match appears.

Brand Management

Clients draw positive associations from a well-managed brand. It is one of the most powerful benefits a broker can provide agents. But when agents are responsible for their own marketing, they are likely to veer away from official brand guidelines. When agents craft their own brand, it is not always intended to work in tandem with the broker's brand. Both scenarios create a conflicting and confusing message to the consumer, ultimately downgrading the quality of the broker's brand. By bringing custom marketing services in-house, the broker creates more cohesion, consistency and, ultimately, a more appealing, effective brand for all.

Scaling Brand Awareness

Brokerages are limited by how much they can spend on marketing. By crafting custom agent brands and extending those elements to templates such as postcards and templates, agents take ownership over their designs and are more likely to spend money growing their brand. The more the agent advertises, the more the brokerage benefits.

Fully Expressing Brand Vision

Brokerages who have adopted the customer-centric model need to consider all the ways they can express that vision and solve agents' greatest challenges. This may come in the form of training and coaching, information technology troubleshooting and transaction management, but it can also be expressed by increasing the level of marketing support. The more the brokerage can deliver on its brand vision, the more that agents can focus on buying and selling, and the more successful the brokerage becomes.

There is also significant risk to this strategy: Custom design services can be very expensive. The salary requirements for a custom marketing team can give a brokerage pause. A chicken-and-egg dilemma emerges: A company may believe that custom design services will generate additional revenue but cannot afford to hire a team before it has the revenue in hand.

Small brokerages rarely have the income to afford this strategy while large brokerages must find ways to justify the additional expense without significantly altering agent compensation plans. When laid out on paper, these reasons make it difficult for a brokerage to commit to a custom marketing service strategy. There is no doubt that jumpstarting this strategy takes initial investment, a clear, organized plan and a focus on the long-term goal.

Of the nine companies who offer custom marketing services T3 Sixty analyzed for this chapter, none are considering eliminating the service, and all recommend it to other companies. They have overcome the financial challenge with a long-term vision and investment, and, as a result, recognized the benefits of the strategy almost immediately.

> "The more the brokerage can deliver on its brand vision, the more that agents can focus on buying and selling."

Evolving Into Design Services

Starting up a custom design services department can come in stages. A full-fledged team is not necessarily required at the outset. Instead, the department can evolve and grow over time, which can be expressed in three stages: templates, freelance and staff.

Templates

Before offering fully customized marketing services, design templates may meet the needs of most organizations. Many brokerages and franchises offer their own template-management platforms. Technology providers also offer this service, including Imprev (imprev.com), Sharper Agent (sharperagent.com) and Inkswitch MarketSpace (inkswitch.com). These platforms allow agents to adjust predefined elements within templates – usually photos, copy and a select set of fonts – without necessarily involving a design team. Final layouts can be automatically sent to a printer that can handle final production and all facets of direct mail.

While this do-it-yourself approach solves the needs of most agents and most listings, it is not uncommon for agents to want to adjust those templates, often with the goal of accommodating their own brand. The brokerage can work with the template vendor to create custom layouts, but this can be time-consuming and expensive. At this juncture, the brokerage may consider advancing to the next step in the evolution of developing an in-house custom marketing department.

Freelance Designer

When agents feel strongly that they need more than templates, they may establish a relationship with a freelance designer who can design templated or customized materials on demand. Brokerages can leverage these relationships and vet designers to help connect them with more agents.

Ideally, the designer is already familiar with the brand and can fully grasp how it is expressed in different media. Freelancers should have the bandwidth to take on more projects as they arise and should be strong communicators since they will most likely be working off-site. The use of a freelance designer carries less risk than taking on a full-time employee, especially if the brokerage is still piloting its marketing programs. As needs grow, more freelancers can be hired to provide flexibility and scalability.

It is best to have a member of the brokerage's staff coordinate the relationship between the agent and the freelance designer. Direct communication between agent and designer can go awry quickly as explained later in the chapter.

Staff

As agents discover the benefits of a skilled designer, more will begin using custom design services, presenting brokerages the opportunity to bring a designer on staff to support them. Full-time staff members are dedicated to delivering on the company's service-centric strategy, and they can simultaneously manage and improve the broker's brand.

Creating the Structure

As with all new initiatives, execution is critical to success and agent adoption. There are many ways to establish a successful custom marketing department. Tactics can vary based upon the specific needs of the organization. There are, however, best practices that brokerages can employ to overcome some of the challenges. Three effective practices include: leadership, staff and agent liaisons.

Leadership

When crafting custom design services, it is important to identify the department leader early in the process. This person needs to have strong project- and people-management skills to effectively balance the needs of agents with the creative team's workload. They should either have prior experience managing a large number of projects or have the capacity to learn along the way. In some cases, this may be a current staff member or even an agent. In most cases, department heads should not work as graphic designers; their focus should be on longer-term vision, strategy and customer service, not the execution of specific projects. Typically, it is most efficient to hire someone who has experience as an account manager at an advertising or design firm.

Staff

Whether starting with a freelance professional or a full-time employee, brokerages need to hire staff members with certain skill sets. Several of the key roles and ideal skills are outlined below.

- **Graphic artists:** These roles should be filled by design specialists, particularly in print. It is also best that they have experience in online design, although digital specialists can be hired separately.

- **Client liaisons:** In small organizations, the department head can work directly with agents. As the company grows, account managers work as client liaisons and project managers to focus on client customer service (see below for more details).

- **Developers:** Coders can help maintain and build new functionality into websites.

- **Copywriters:** Copywriters craft copy for agent bios, websites, flyers, ads and high-end property listings.

- **Marketing specialists:** Digital marketing is becoming evermore important in real estate branding. These specialists optimize and maintain social media profiles and search engine optimized pages, design and run advertising campaigns and more.

The staff needs to possess common skills, such as:

- A positive demeanor that allows them to work well with a diverse and demanding set of agents.

- Graphic designers should have a well-honed and flexible skill set. This allows them to work with a variety of media, including print and online, each of which each requires a specific approach to design (although hiring specialists in each medium helps to resolve this issue).

- It is best if all marketing staff have a strong understanding of the residential real estate industry. It is important to understand the needs of agents, grasp the buying and selling process and proactively plan for the challenges agents may not be aware of. If staff members do not already have this knowledge, the onboarding process can take longer.

After the department head, the first hire in the department should be a graphic designer because so much of the work — flyers, postcards, image retouching — is visual in nature. Departments can then scale by adding graphic designers, account managers, production managers and copywriters

"Large organizations. which have over 2,000 agents, have gone so far as to employ social media specialists, developers and data scientists."

Agent Liaisons

Marketing departments differ on who should work directly with agents. They typically structure the department in one of two ways: designers work directly with agents or they work through an account manager who interfaces with agents.

The former setup relies heavily on design team staff. They need to consistently deliver high-quality work within short timeframes while having the patience to work with agents who may frequently change their minds. People with these capabilities are hard to come by. But smaller brokerages will likely go this route to keep costs and head counts low, adding management staff as they scale.

Having account managers that serve as the go-between agents and the creative team can have multiple benefits: the account rep can focus on strategy, customer service and project management. Professional advertising and design firms are traditionally structured this way. While this is beneficial for agents and the marketing team, this structure increases head count and department costs, and is typically only feasible for larger brokerages or those in luxury markets.

Strategic Decisions

When establishing an in-house design department, brokerages need to make some important decisions at the outset.

To Charge or Not to Charge

Brokerages differ on charging agents for design services. The marketing department is rarely considered a profit center, so agent fees, if any, are kept low to encourage adoption. As a result, the company maintains a high level of quality. There are three approaches to charging agents for design services:

- No fees are charged.

- Agents are charged for the designer's time, but there is no upcharge. The brokerage typically negotiates low rates with freelancers so costs are far less than an outside vendor.

- Most brokerages charge low fees that do not cover expenses. This prevents agents from misusing the marketing department's time. Based on T3 Sixty's interviews with brokerages with custom design services, sample charges include: $360 for a logo; $30 per hour for a logo; $45 per hour in-house for copywriting; a new logo is free, with changes to an existing logo costing $25; a personal or property video is $285 (through an in-house production team).

Most brokerages shy away from launching custom marketing services because the department is not a profit center and requires significant investment. However, all nine brokerages interviewed for this chapter stated that the benefits far outweighed the costs.

Death by a Thousand Tweaks

In the world of advertising and design, the best creative strategies "dance on the head of a pin," as the saying goes. In other words, the more precisely the audience and unique selling propositions are defined, the more impactful the marketing will be.

Real estate agents come from diverse backgrounds, and therefore most of them do not have the ability to know exactly what they want from marketing. If they do not know how to manage the process, countless tweaks of each design element can derail the project. This can be unproductive and may prevent completion of the project, amounting to wasted time, effort and capital.

It is the marketing team's responsibility to extract the information it needs from agents by asking the right questions. This may take the form of a conversation between agents and the marketing representative or through a questionnaire, which is particularly helpful for brokerages with larger agent counts (see sidebar). Either way, project management skills are critical to success.

Logo and Brand Questionnaire

When starting work on an agent's brand, it is critical to get a clear understanding of his or her needs and expectations. T3 Sixty recommends asking the following questions:

What key messages do you want your brand to communicate?

Do you prefer your brand to be modern, traditional or some combination of the two? Do you prefer more photography and less text, or vice versa? People may have different interpretations of the same phrase, so use examples to get a better understanding of their preferences.

Which logos, brands and colors appeal to you?

To exemplify agents' vision, ask them to add images to a Pinterest board. Meet with them so they can explain their reasoning. After refining this collection of images, it becomes a mood board, a common touch point that reflects the new brand's style, colors, emotions, tones and textures. This helps designers consistently express the brand across multiple media. However, agents should be reminded that final artwork may be restricted by the brokerage's brand guidelines.

Are there images you wish to include or avoid?

Low-quality images (e.g., stock photography) can downgrade the perceived value of a brand. Use images carefully and sparingly, keeping them in line with the brand's overall standards.

Are there any other assets you would like to include, such as a tagline or designations?

These questions are good to ask upfront to avoid shoehorning preferences in at a later date.

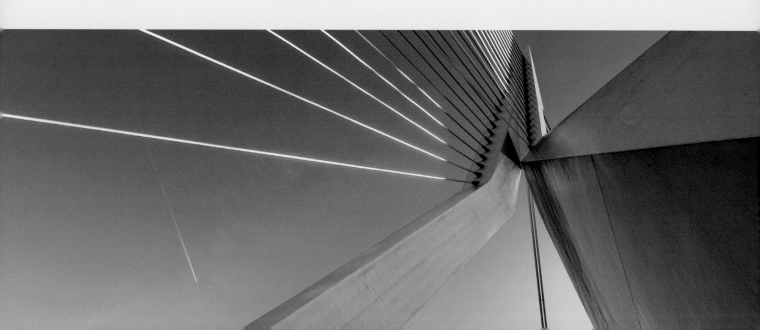

Who Benefits?

Companies are split on how to offer custom marketing services to their agent corps. They typically approach this issue from two perspectives: making these services available only to top producers, or making them available to all their agents. Both strategies are discussed below.

The top producer approach
Some brokerages believe that only top producers – and agents who may soon become top producers – should receive the marketing team's time and attention. On one hand, top producers are more likely to need and use personalized branding materials. The department's time is usually in limited supply, so the brokerage benefits by spending its time on projects that are most likely to deliver the greatest return. On the other hand, the remaining agents – who make up the majority of the brokerage – do not have access to the service. This can make them feel like the company is not willing to invest in their businesses. Management often takes a flexible approach to this policy, providing customization services to agents who want it most.

The egalitarian approach
Some companies offer custom design services to all their agents. Although this requires a high staff-to-agent ratio, it can exemplify an organization's dedication to helping everyone succeed. As a result, agents establish a strong connection with the brokerage, which can lead to long-term growth for agent and broker alike.

How to Say No

Personal brands often leverage the brokerage's brand, but this can be a slippery slope. Without careful management, agents will begin to push boundaries, which can lead to inconsistent marketing quality for the company as a whole.

The most direct way to maintain a consistent brand experience across a wide array of agent brands is to create a brand guidelines document. Most companies already have this, as it defines how marketing assets such as logo, color palette and fonts can or cannot be used. Even with well-defined brand guidelines, it is important for the company to be willing to say no to agent requests. Some even require that agents recite a pledge that they will not vary from brand standards. However, many agents are proud of their company's brand, and if management has earned their respect, they are almost always willing to comply with company policy.

Execution is the Key to Adoption

The larger a marketing department becomes, the harder it can be to manage a large number of projects. Without proper leadership and staff, the team can become overwhelmed. Longer-term projects are placed behind more immediate needs like weekend open houses, which can lead to growing agent dissatisfaction. This is particularly challenging when the marketing department is a distributed team. But by leveraging communication and technology tools, these issues can be greatly alleviated if not resolved altogether.

Marketing teams at larger organizations use project management platforms such as Hive (hive.com), Wrike (wrike.com), Smartsheet (smartsheet.com) and ShopVOX (shopvox.com) Many of these platforms offer front-end interfaces or application programming interfaces (APIs), which allow agents to order and track projects through a company portal or intranet.

Driving Adoption

As detailed in the 2017 Swanepoel Trends Report, agent adoption of broker services can be a significant challenge. However, the marketing department has an advantage: Many agents consider marketing a critical element in their day-to-day success. From listing and buyer presentations to brochures and single-property websites, agents can draw a direct line between quality marketing and business growth.

To encourage companywide adoption, management should create a rollout plan. This requires announcements at each office and ongoing engagement from office leaders. Brokerages can further encourage agents to use their marketing services through a combination of low pricing, high-quality materials, ease of use and management support. If adoption rates slow, the marketing department can reach out to agents on a one-on-one basis.

Over time, agents naturally gravitate to in-house marketing without much prodding, which helps build a bond between agents and brokerage. As more agents successfully use the offerings, it draws the attention of others, who in turn will find more ways to use it. This virtuous circle is valuable for both the company and agents.

Tracking Success

Once a brokerage launches design services, it should keep track of which tools drive success. Unfortunately, brokerages often manage this in a haphazard way; anecdotal conversations or complaints at a sales meeting are not necessarily the right impetus for change. Instead, a structured and qualitative approach is more beneficial. Common key performance indicators (KPIs) include agent adoption rates and return on investment. Over time, the brokerage can determine what initiatives are working well and those that need to be revamped or retired.

When launching a new service, the department may elect to work with a select group of forward-thinking agents willing to be part of a beta test. In return for receiving advanced access to a new tool, they report back on KPIs such as listing and buyer presentations won and lost, website visits, leads generated and converted and, ultimately, ROI.

Takeaway

Many brokerages offer agents a fairly basic operational platform. However, an increasing number are adopting a service-centric model, offering a higher and more customized level of service to their agents. This strategy has become so common in certain major metropolitan markets that brokerages now need to do more to differentiate themselves from their competition. As brokerages search for new ways to achieve this goal, we expect more will begin offering their agents custom design services.

Today, the brokerages who offer custom design services are also primarily based in major markets where they serve more demanding clients and agents. However, few brokers offer the levels of service described in this chapter – this is still very new in most markets.

If brokers have the financial means, which can be difficult in low-margin business models and geographies, there is tremendous opportunity to be the first to offer these custom design services. This strategy, however, also faces challenges: Finding the right personnel, scaling efficiently as the company grows and delivering ROI take diligent work and are critical to success.

An evolution in real estate marketing will create new opportunities for marketing agencies that can meet the specific needs of brokerages. Companies such as Agent Operations (agentoperations.net) are already experiencing success with this strategy; Agent Operations has more than doubled in size each year for the past three years, for example. Brokerages, such as M Realty in Portland, Oregon, and Seven Gables (sevengables.com) in Orange County, California, are spinning out their marketing services and offering them to agents at other brokerages. Marketing vendors will find success when they combine a strong understanding of the unique real estate category with competitive pricing.

Custom marketing services are not only an expression of a brokerage's brand but a promise to support and grow its agents. The challenge brokers face involves executing well without creating significant burden on the bottom line.

05

Brokerage M&A Momentum Broadens

Tier 2 Firms Now Expanding Through Large Acquisitions

The residential real estate brokerage business is maturing from a mom-and-pop industry into a sophisticated corporate-managed industry. While the industry's largest firms, which we call Tier 1 companies, have been the dominant players in large M&A activity, they are no longer the only ones using acquisitions to grow. This shift has significant ramifications for the industry, which we examine in this chapter.

Mergers and Acquisitions

Before we dive in, we will first define a few phrases and concepts. A merger is the process of combining two companies into a new one. An acquisition involves one company purchasing and absorbing another, although at times the purchased company may continue to exist as a separate brand.

There are two types of M&As: horizontal, where two competitors come together, and vertical, where non-competitors in related vertical markets combine strengths. This chapter focuses on the former.

Standard business strategy dictates that to become more profitable, a company must either increase revenues while keeping costs in check, or reduce costs while maintaining revenue. While not as common, defensive factors can also spur M&A. This includes increasing the size of the company to make it less susceptible to acquisition itself, to fight off new competitors who pose a threat to a smaller firm, or as a hedge against a changing business environment. In most cases, companies pursue M&As to increase profit.

Increased M&A continues the real estate brokerage industry's decades-long march toward maturation.

The Brokerage Landscape

Historically, three words can best be used to describe the residential real estate brokerage industry: Small, local and independent. Consider these statistics from the National Association of Realtors 2017 Profile of Real Estate Firms:

- Seventy-nine percent of real estate firms have a single office, typically with three full-time real estate licensees.

- Eighty-four percent of firms are independent non-franchised firms, and 13 percent are independent franchised firms.

- Twenty-six percent of firms are sole proprietorships, 36 percent are LLCs, 27 percent are S-Corps, and 9 percent are C-Corps.

- Fifty-seven percent of firms work in metro areas and 30 percent work in a rural area or small town, 7 percent cover a resort area or small town, and 5 percent cover a multi-state area. Only 1 percent are nationwide firms.

- Firms with only one office have a median of 20 transactions with an annual sales volume of $4.3 million. Conversely, firms with four or more offices are significantly larger with a median of 550 annual transactions and a median annual sales volume of $235 million.

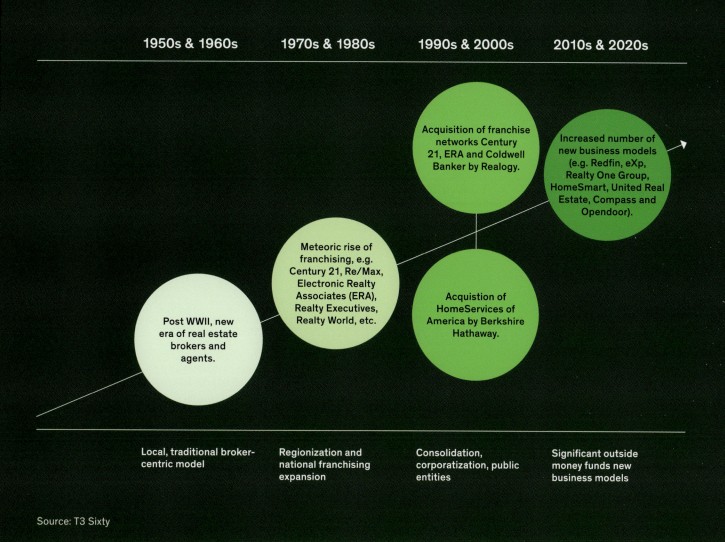

These numbers clearly reflect the industry's large number of mom-and-pop brokerages. Industry veterans content to be working brokers, managing a few agents and their own book of business primarily operate these firms. They are the bedrock of an industry that has incredibly low barriers to entry; by aggregating listing data in a local MLS, these small firms have a place in the market.

There is, of course, a more corporate side of the business. Big brokerage companies, both franchised and nonfranchised, have strong brand presence and represent a large percentage of the market. These include companies such as Re/Max, Keller Williams Realty, the Realogy brands (Coldwell Banker, Century 21, Sotheby's Realty, ERA Real Estate and Better Homes and Gardens).

Real Estate Brokerages Dissected

To help the industry get its head around the entire real estate brokerage community, T3 Sixty developed a categorization of brokerages by size. To do this, T3 Sixty studied the 2017 Real Trends 500, 2017 RISMedia Power Broker list, 2017 NAR Profile of Real Estate Firms, the most recent U.S. Census (2012), T3 Sixty's own broker database and spoke with many of the executives at the country's largest real estate brokerages.

T3 Sixty Real Estate Brokerage Tiers

Group	Category	Tier	Annual Sales Volume	Number of Firms	Description
Mega Brokers	The Titans	Tier 1	($100 billion plus)	2 firms	The Titans do more than $100 billion in annual sales.
Mega Brokers	Power Brokers	Tier 2	($5 billion – $100 billion)	30 firms	Power Brokers represent the top 1,000 brokerage companies in the country. Firms in this group have annual sales volumes of over $500 million and have been divided into four tiers.
Mega Brokers	Power Brokers	Tier 3	($2 billion – $5 billion)	100 firms	
Mega Brokers	Power Brokers	Tier 4	($1 billion – $2 billion)	260 firms	
Mega Brokers	Power Brokers	Tier 5	($500 million – $1 billion)	600 firms	
Large Brokers	Local Brokers	Tier 6	($100 million – $500 million)	5,000 firms	Local Brokers have annual sales volumes of over $25 million and is the group for which the least amount of accurate and complete data could be found. T3 Sixty hopes to do more research on this large and important group of companies in the not-too-distant future. These firms have been divided into three tiers.
Large Brokers	Local Brokers	Tier 7	($50 million – $100 million)	5,000 firms	
Large Brokers	Local Brokers	Tier 8	($25 million – $50 million)	10,000 firms	
Small Brokers	The Rest	Tier 9	(up to $25 million)	60,000 firms	This enormous group represents the remaining 65,000 real estate brokerage firms. They include the single-broker shops, the mom-and-pop firms, the part-timers and those who recently started and are on their way up. While making up the lion's share of actual firms, they represent a small fraction of the industry's sales volume.
Small Brokers	The Rest	Tier 10	(zero sales)	5,000 firms	

Source: T3 Sixty
Notes:
The tiers were created to facilitate understanding not to brand any company.
The number of firms in each tier were rounded off to simplify understanding.
Numbers in parentheses represents average annual sales volume for each respective tier.

The Titans

While the industry consists of approximately 86,000 brokerage companies representing approximately 11 million annual transaction sides, the top two brokerage companies – Realogy's NRT LLC (nrtllc.com) and Berkshire Hathaway's HomeServices of America (homeservices.com) – collectively account for approximately 6 percent of the national residential real estate market share based on transaction volume (this accounting reflects company-owned brokerage production, not of the franchises associated with these companies).

National Real Estate Trust (NRT)

Created in 1996, NRT is the nation's largest residential real estate brokerage company. A subsidiary of Realogy, it owns and operates brokerage firms in more than 50 of the U.S.'s 100 largest metropolitan areas. Realogy-predecessor HFS Incorporated created NRT when it purchased Coldwell Banker Corporation in 1996 and wanted it to remain a franchisor. NRT's initial purpose centered on owning the nearly 400 brokerage offices acquired in the Coldwell Banker purchase. Since its formation, NRT has been an active acquirer of real estate firms both large and small.

Today, the majority of NRT firms fly under the Realogy-owned Coldwell Banker and Sotheby's International Realty flags, but NRT also owns and operates independent brands such as Corcoran Group in New York City and Climb Real Estate in San Francisco.

In an industry where the majority of brokerage companies consist of one office with a median of 20 annual transaction sides and $4.3 million in annual sales volume, NRT's numbers are staggering. With 47,500 agents operating out of 789 offices, it will close over 340,000 transaction sides for a total of $166 billion in 2017.

HomeServices of America (HSA)

Billing itself as "Local Real Estate Nationwide," HSA has been the solid No. 2 player behind NRT for years. That gap shrunk significantly in 2017 with its acquisition of the nation's third-largest brokerage, Long & Foster Real Estate (longandfoster.com), and another top 10 brokerage, Houlihan Lawrence (houlihanlawrence.com). These acquisitions put HSA's 2016 numbers almost on par with NRT's. Nearly identical in transaction sides at 340,000 and about 25 percent behind in sales volume (at $125 billion). At 826, HSA has a few more offices, but at 41,000 agents, has approximately 13 percent less agents.

The difference between Tier 1 companies NRT and HSA and the rest of the real estate brokerage landscape is significant. With nearly 100,000 agents operating in over 1,500 offices, NRT and HSA will transact approximately

700,000 sides in 2017. This is roughly 20 percent more transaction sides than the rest of the top 25 firms combined.

Another way to appreciate the size difference of Tier 1 firms from the rest of the field is to compare them with the next-largest firms. Each Tier 1 company has 260,000 more transaction sides than the largest Tier 2 firm, and 330,000 more transaction sides than the smallest Tier 2 firm.

At its core, real estate is a simple business. Confined by thin margins, successful firms recruit producing agents, retain those agents with a competitive value proposition and efficiently manage costs to maximize profit. With these limitations, significantly increasing net profit at the margin has historically been difficult. The most direct way for a large firm to increase profit is

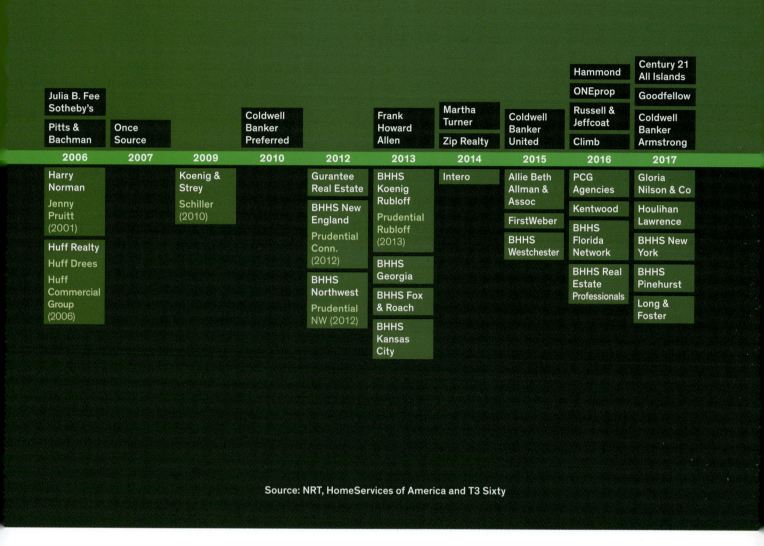

to acquire market share in large chunks. Both NRT and HSA have used this strategy to separate themselves from the rest of the industry.

Despite the impressive size of Tier 1 brokerages, however, the residential real estate brokerage industry remains well-segmented and far from consolidated.

Power Brokers

The Power Brokers are often described as the industry's thoroughbreds. This category includes approximately 1,000 companies that each transact between $500 million and $100 billion in annual sales volume. As this is a large spread, the category is organized into four tiers (see table).

Tier 2 firms sit atop the Power Broker group. Based on reported 2016 sales numbers and projected 2017 numbers (final sales 2017 numbers aren't usually available until around April 2018), the following firms make up most of Tier 2:

Howard Hanna Real Estate (howardhanna.com)[1]

Douglas Elliman (elliman.com)

Weichert Realtors (weichert.com)[1]

Pacific Union (pacificunion.com)[1]

Realty One Group (realtyonegroup.com)

Alain Pinel Realtors (apr.com)

William Raveis Real Estate (raveis.com)

Compass (compass.com)

HomeSmart International (homesmart.com)[1]

@properties (atproperties.com)

Keller Williams Realty GO Management[2]

Ebby Halliday Real Estate (ebby.com)

Re/Max Equity Group (equitygroup.com)

John L. Scott Real Estate (johnlscott.com)

Coldwell Banker Bain/Seal (coldwellbankerbain.com)

First Team Real Estate (firstteam.com)

Keller Williams Realty Forward Management[2]

Re/Max Results (results.net)

Allen Tate Companies (allentate.com)

Real Estate One (realestateone.com)

LIV Sotheby's International Realty (livsothebysrealty.com)

Baird & Warner (bairdwarner.com)

Crye-Leike Realtors (crye-leike.com)[1]

Rodeo Realty (rodeore.com)

Notes

[1] These companies own franchise and company-owned stores.
[2] These KW management companies own and operate multiple market center and therefore have multiple websites.
Although Long & Foster and Houlihan Lawrence would qualify, they were both acquired by Berkshire Hathaway HomeServices of America in 2017 and therefore are no longer listed independently.
Companies with more franchise or affiliated sales, rather than company-owned stores, such as Windermere Real Estate (windermere.com) are not included.

In most cases, a Tier 2 Power Broker is one of the largest players in its respective market. In the country's top 100 metro areas, an NRT or HomeServices of America company, or one of the major franchises, Coldwell Banker, Re/Max or Keller Williams Realty round out the top three in major metropolitan areas..

Wall Street dollars have, in the past, provided Tier 1 brokerage firms the investment capital to fuel their national acquisition strategy. Power Brokers, on the other hand, have historically been funded through their owners and grew organically in different ways. However, many ended up with comparable operational structures and needs, so they tend to budget along similar lines, have similar best practices and allocate comparable resources to their businesses. Over time, they have grown to be friends, colleagues and competitors, and have learned from each other. Through these relationships, Power Brokers have grown by acquiring local competitors who are of much smaller size than the acquisitions Tier 1 firms typically make.

Recently, however, Tier 2 companies are now using M&A of large competitors to expand outside of their traditional local territories with acquisitions of Big Broker (Tier 6 to 8) firms. Below are some of the prominent Power Brokers who have pursued large out-of-market M&As over the past 24 months.

Howard Hanna Real Estate
Based in Pittsburgh, Howard Hanna Real Estate is a third-generation family business with approximately 8,000 agents, $18 billion in annual sales and operations in eight states. Like many large brokerage firms, it has grown by acquiring relatively small firms within its historical core Northeast market.

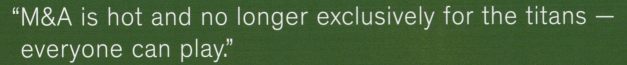

"M&A is hot and no longer exclusively for the titans — everyone can play."

It has expanded its growth strategy in the last few years by acquiring significantly larger companies. In 2014, Howard Hanna acquired William E. Wood, a preeminent firm in southeast Virginia and coastal North Carolina. At the time, William E. Wood was a local market power with 700 agents and $1.5 billion in annual sales. While the acquisition itself was noteworthy due to its size, the firm's location, far outside of the historical Howard Hanna market area of Pennsylvania and Ohio, indicated a different and bolder growth strategy.

The following year in 2015, Howard Hanna acquired Nothnagle Realtors (nothnagle.com) and its 770 agents, 32 offices, $1.4 billion in annual sales volume and nearly 10,000 annual transaction sides. Howard Hanna followed this with an acquisition of RealtyUSA (realtyusa.com) in 2016; with 65 offices and more than 2,200 agents, RealtyUSA was the largest real estate broker in New York state and the eighth largest real estate company in the country by transaction sides. Although Nothnagle and RealtyUSA initially operated under their brands, Howard Hanna brought them under its brand in 2017.

Howard Hanna is now looking to make more acquisitions east of the Mississippi, according to Howard Hanna President Hoby Hanna. Howard Hanna prefers to grow in contiguous areas (or those relatively near its core operating area) as it has a high-touch acquisition strategy. Culture and leadership trump financials for the firm when evaluating potential acquisition targets. Because most agents at the firms it acquires are independent contractors, strong culture and leadership ensure the firm can stay steady through the readjustment that accompanies an acquisition.

Douglas Elliman
New York City real estate has always operated in its own universe. With no MLS, virtually no Realtor association presence and most of the market consisting of rentals, it is unlike any other market in the country. Hence, national firms and franchises have generally struggled to enter this market that has been predominantly controlled by local independents, particularly Corcoran Group (corcoran.com, acquired by NRT in 2001) and Douglas Elliman.

Douglas Elliman reflects the Big Apple's corporate character with a variety of investment entity owners. With nearly $25 billion in annual sales volume, it has grown into one of the five largest real estate companies in the country. Although primarily a New York City-based operation, Elliman ventured south to Florida in 2011. While straying from its New York roots, this move was a natural market expansion based on the historical migration of city dwellers to the Sunshine State.

Elliman has continued its out-of-state expansion plan since then. In 2017, it jumped the entire country with the purchase of Los Angeles-based brokerage Teles Properties (telesproperties.com). With the addition of Teles' 21 offices and 630 agents in Southern California (and its Colorado presence of five offices and 58 associates), Elliman became one of the largest brokerage firms in California. It also plans to expand to Massachusetts by the end of 2017. With a bicoastal footprint, the brokerage is well-positioned to grow further.

Pacific Union Real Estate

San Francisco Bay Area powerhouse Pacific Union Real Estate has been in growth mode since CEO Mark McLaughlin acquired it in 2009. In 2016, it acquired the well-known Southern California luxury firm John Aaroe Group (aaroe.com), which made Pacific Union a California regional brokerage with more than 1,100 agents working in 38 offices. In 2017, the company acquired Southern California-based Partners Trust (thepartnerstrust.com) and its 240 agents. Late in 2017, it acquired a majority stake in Los Angeles-based luxury brokerage Gibson International, which does approximately $1 billion in annual sales volume.

With 47 offices and more than 1,400 agents, Pacific Union has become one of the largest real estate brokerages in California. The publicly traded multi-discipline real estate juggernaut Fidelity National Financial (fnf.com) owns a majority stake in the firm.

What's Driving Out-of-Market Acquisitions?

Local vs. National

NRT and HSA are the only true national residential real estate brokerage companies. While they have national headquarters (New Jersey and Minnesota for NRT and HSA, respectively), they are brokerage conglomerates with businesses focused on growth and expansion. All indications suggest that this acquisition strategy will continue and possibly even increase in pace.

However, nearly every other brokerage firm is different from these national players. The majority of brokerages began as businesses with local roots in local markets, and in almost all cases their local presence is still critical to their operations. This is true even for Power Brokers. For example, Howard Hanna is entrenched in Pittsburgh (now with offices in all of Ohio, Pennsylvania, New York, Michigan, Virginia, North Carolina, West Virginia, and Maryland), Pacific Union in the San Francisco Bay Area (now offices throughout California), Douglas Elliman in New York City (now offices all over New York, New Jersey, Connecticut, South Florida and recently California and Colorado).

A Simple Game

At its core, the real estate brokerage industry is a market demand-servicing business. Competitors duel in a relatively simple zero-sum game of market share attraction and retention. There was a time when real estate brokers owned the customer relationship. Those days are long gone, perhaps with the exception of new-era discount brokerage models as discussed in Trend No. 3, "Rise of the Modern Day Brokerage."

Even though the brokerage company is the legal entity through which a seller or buyer creates an agency relationship, real estate agents develop the actual business relationship. Acknowledging this, most successful brokerage firms have relied on the two-prong strategy of recruiting producing agents who bring valuable relationships with them and attracting new agents to the business, some of whom will become top producers while others pay fees before dropping out. Traditionally, brokerages accomplish this with aggressive branch managers who are constantly looking for talent and the occasional in-market acquisition of a smaller competitor.

By all accounts, Tier 2 real estate brokerage firms such as Howard Hanna, Douglas Elliman and Pacific Union have all been incredibly successful at growing in their local regions through traditional means: increasing profits by growing revenue and reducing costs.

> "The residential real estate brokerage industry has matured and evolved into an era of professional management."

Local Revenue Growth Has Limits

A brokerage firm can grow revenue in several ways. The most direct route is through an increase in gross commission income from its affiliated agents. This can involve increasing agent production, which can be difficult due to agents' independent contractor status. It can also involve taking market share from local competitors by recruiting their agents.

While new agents join brokerages on a regular basis, producing agents tend not to move to other companies once they are established in the business. There are various reasons for this.

First, many producing agents have longstanding relationships with their current firms and, while some may scoff at the notion that their firm affiliation is not meaningful, many are fearful of a brand change. This is especially true in a healthy market. Good and top producing agents are careful to avoid doing anything that could negatively affect their business, and when business is going well a brand change adds an unknown variable into that equation.

Also, many producing agents have negotiated special commission split deals with smaller firms. A move to a larger firm may not yield the same benefits. The difficulty of recruiting agents from firms once they grow to a certain size, especially if they become a market leader, reflects this fact.

It is far more difficult for a market-leading firm to grow its local market share from 15 percent to 20 percent through traditional agent recruiting channels than it is for that same firm to enter a new market by acquiring an existing firm with 5 percent market share.

A New-Found Focus on Scale

Topline revenue growth is a key driver of M&A activity, and so is the other side of the ledger: reducing costs. Technology plays a huge role here.
A discussion of real estate today necessarily includes the topic of technology. One of technology's core benefits, especially in terms of costs, is scalability. As this chapter makes clear, most real estate brokerage firms are small, which means they miss out on the benefits of scale. Larger firms like Tier 2 Power Brokers are beginning to understand, and harness, the power of scale through technology and its positive impact on reducing operational costs.

For example, in the past, processing real estate transactions required significant human capital, the most expensive cost on a brokerage's profit and loss statement. Receiving listing and transaction documents, reviewing them, issuing and updating commission disbursement authorizations, collecting commissions, paying vendors, ensuring agents are paid timely and accurately and then connecting it all in the accounting department can, without appropriate systems, be a daisy-chain of human inefficiency and cost.

One of the technology advancements brokers now enjoy include significant advances in back-office transaction processing that greatly streamline and automate the scenario described above. The systems can easily, and cheaply, handle greater volume; while, in the human-centered past, growth would have come at great expense. Human oversight and involvement will always be required, but the more that firms can leverage scalable technology solutions, the more efficiently they process transactions at lower costs and higher profits.

Takeaway

Brokerage M&A activity in 2016 and 2017 has been higher than any year in the last decade. When HomeServices of America acquired Long & Foster, it joined NRT in the Titan category ($100 billion annual sales volume). 2017 also brought blockbuster transactions including acquisitions of large regional firms such as Houlihan Lawrence, Partners Trust and Teles Properties. This momentum suggests the residential real estate brokerage industry may have a prolific 2018 ahead.

2017 also made it clear that ambitious and substantial mergers and acquisitions are no longer restricted to Tier 1 national brokerage companies. More companies are finding value in this growth strategy, and Tier 2 brokerages are taking the lead. As Tier 2 companies step up their M&A activity, they significantly expand the pool of brokerage buyers.

As many Mega Broker owners reach the twilight of their career with few natural succession options in many cases, M&A becomes an increasingly viable exit strategy. As more sell and join even larger powerhouses, a new group of ambitious newcomers will move up the ranks.

Gone are the days when an agent or founding entrepreneur is the only or best person to run the company. The residential real estate brokerage industry has matured and evolved into an era of professional management. For more detail on this professional management trend, see Trend No. 4, "The Management-Empowered Business Model."

As the saying goes, "Time waits for no one." Mega Brokers, who have watched some of these acquisition stories unfold nationally and even in their own markets, are rightly asking, "Who's next?"

This trend will continue. Therefore, smart Mega Brokers should be analyzing where they might fit into the local, regional and national M&A landscape. At the core of this analysis is how brokerage firms become stronger, generate more revenue, lowers their cost structure and generate more profit from acquisitions. That holds true for both the acquirer and acquiree. M&A is certainly not an appropriate course for every firm, but even if Mega Brokers do not determine it to be an appropriate strategy, they should prepare for M&A to affect them in their local market.

Professional Support by a Powerful Ally

T3 Mergers + Acquisitions

- Company Valuations
- Business Packaging
- Market Analysis
- Presentation Development
- Scenario Planning
- Evaluation of Options
- Seller Representation
- Negotiations

t360.com

04

The Management-Empowered Brokerage Business Model

As the Industry Matures, so Must Management

Over the past decade, the quickening pace of technological change, the growing power of the real estate consumer, and the rapidly expanding role of data have fundamentally altered the real estate landscape. The past several editions of the Swanepoel Trends Report have monitored a series of important industry changes including new ways to market listings, capture consumer attention and stay in touch with consumers. This is not just a series of independent trends; taken together, they demonstrate an underlying shift that has significant impact on the traditional brokerage business model and paves the way for the real estate business model of tomorrow we call the Management-Empowered Brokerage. We outline in this chapter how and why brokerages need to implement this structure into their design to thrive in this new, emerging environment.

This chapter was inspired by Jeremy Conaway, who contributed significantly to it. Sections of the chapter were sourced from projects that he manages outside of real estate. T3 Sixty decided to include significant parts of this research with minor retooling as it strongly applies to the current residential real estate brokerage landscape. Jeremy has been a long-time contributing editor for the Swanepoel Trends Report.

Replacing the Traditional Brokerage Model

The current real estate business model, often referred to as the traditional model, has enjoyed a long and successful run since the post-World War II economic boom. It has contributed to a stable industry, even through the emergence of the agent power movement in the 1990s, advanced technologies in the 2000s, and the empowered consumer in the 2010s. It has even continued to show vitality through the growth of big data in the first half of this decade.

But fatigue is growing. As has been the case in virtually every other industry since 2010, a constant stream of disruptive trends is destabilizing the traditional business model by offering consumers new ways to transact. Now the traditional real estate business model faces irrelevance.

What's Driving The Change?

A number of elements spell the traditional real estate business model's demise. They are listed below.

Management Limitations

Managers of traditional brokerages have limited ability to truly control their organizations, which is becoming a significant shortcoming. As a result, brokerages cannot deliver a minimum level of acceptable service to consumers. Even though managers, from franchisors to brokerages to department heads, have tried their best to institute changes in efficiency, effectiveness and relevancy, they usually struggle.

Agent-Centricity

When brokerages consider real estate agents their ultimate beneficiary and customer, they find it difficult to focus on consumers, optimize companywide technologies, create more efficient transactions, increase profitability and enhance operations with data. Despite huge investments by brokerages, agents have generally resisted adopting company efforts. The industry's thread of agent-centricity and strong-willed individualism has stymied brokerage management's efforts to institute much-needed changes.

> "This is not fear-mongering, but an insistent plea to brokerage leaders to take an ice-cold shower and look around them with an open mind."

Consumer Expectations

While consumers expect greater transparency and simplicity when they make purchases, the real estate transaction process has become increasingly complex. Operational standards can help close this gap, but brokerages are trapped by an independent contractor-driven system. Without a high level of control, real estate brokerages cannot evolve to create consistent, predictable, great experiences for consumers and their agents. (Leaders of some of the new brokerage models have been able to address this issue by taking a different approach to the broker-agent relationship by paying agents a salary. Although this creates other complexities, it allows them to enforce clearly defined best practices and hold agents accountable.

These factors have put the traditional brokerage model under severe pressure. If shrinking profits, clunky technological compatibility, low valuations by

Wall Street investors and waning appeal among consumers are added in, the traditional model's dire situation becomes even clearer.

Consumer Loyalty

Today's technologically-empowered, internet-savvy consumers (especially millennials) have little loyalty to or use for traditional brokerages. For most consumers, the definition of "Realtor" has no special meaning. They are increasingly aware of the services and pricing offered by new brokerage models, and an increasing number of consumers are migrating to them. (For more see Trend No. 3, "Rise of the Modern Discount Brokerage.")

Venture Capital

Venture capital investors (VCs) also play a big role in the challenges faced by modern brokerages. Over the past three years, VCs and other investors have poured over $3.9 billion into new, alternative or emerging brokerage business models. They are fueling the startups developing the standards, best practices, functionalities, technology and modern business culture discussed in this chapter (For more, see Trend No. 1, "Follow the Money.")

Emerging Technology

Today's real estate marketplace bustles with new technologies that improve transactions and the overall consumer experience. The most successful use innovative technologies and strategies to drive significant growth.

Failure to Respond

For the most part, legacy brokerages have failed to appropriately respond to the threat and opportunity of this new environment. Consider Project Upstream, for example. Brokers specifically developed Upstream to manage their own inventories, but brokers refused to fund the platform's development and the entity they created to represent their interests, UpstreamRE (upstreamre.com). However, they convinced the National Association of Realtors to fund its development and operations. NAR's millions of dollars of investment have given it virtually total control of Upstream, evaporating Upstream's founding goal of giving brokers control of their listings.

Direct Buyer Movement

Emerging Direct Buyers such as Opendoor (opendoor.com) meet the needs of the real estate consumers who want Amazon-like certainty in the price, process and timeline of real estate transactions. (For more, see Trend No. 2, "The Direct Buyer Phenomenon.")

Transition to a Management-Empowered Brokerage Model

To respond to these fundamental changes, the traditional model must evolve. We call the new paradigm the Management-Empowered Brokerage (MEB) model, which professionalizes brokerage operations and creates an operational framework that supports the function as a modern, nimble, digital-age business.

Traditional brokerages were built during and for a different era. These companies are no longer competing with companies playing by those rules or with the same technology or funding. A streamlined professionalization of real estate brokerage operations has never been as important as it is now given the need for speed in adapting to market conditions, the revolution catalyzed by technology and the immense influx in venture capital funding reshaping the industry. Until recently, professional investor money has not been a factor. Now, firms such as Redfin (redfin.com) and Compass (compass.com) are bringing hundreds of millions of investor dollars to the brokerage landscape and using powerful weapons such as websites and mobile apps to the fight for brokerage market share not present a decade ago.

> "An overwhelming percentage of business leaders in other industries have long understood that management must control every aspect of a business for it to succeed and thrive in the long term."

This maturation requires a careful analysis of a company's structure and consumer offering by brokerage leadership. It requires that leaders have a rigorous, unflinching focus on goals, measurement, refinement and accountability in all facets of their business. While it is not easy, it is necessary.

Each brokerage should design its own best practices. Industrywide standards are sparse and mostly unproven. Agents are also a critical component – the Management-Empowered Brokerage model is not a top-down operation; quite the opposite, in fact.

This section outlines the key elements necessary for a successful transition.

Develop an Effective Business Philosophy and Company Culture

Perhaps the most important elements that support a successful MEB are an effective, sustainable business philosophy and company culture.

Business philosophy is the set of beliefs and principles that a brokerage incorporates into the management of its organization. This often takes the form of a mission statement or company vision that guides the firm's decisions, outlook and goals. It essentially functions as the company's operational blueprint, guiding operations that address the needs of the real estate buyer and seller.

Company culture is just as important, if not more so. It brings business philosophy to life. In a thriving business culture, employees feel empowered, communication is clear, roles are well-defined and everyone feels invested in the company's larger vision and vital to executing it.

Without these two key elements clearly defined and cared for, the transition to a MEB model will lack the foundation necessary for success.

Create an Appropriate Management Mindset and Attitude

Management plays a critical role here; company leaders are the root from which operations flow. They set expectations, develop plans to meet goals, set accountability, mentor and provide guidance, and keep the company ship moving forward.

In this model, the company's key players are not individual agents; they are the management team as a whole. Management must build operations that align with and support the culture. They use best practices and standards — created in partnership with agents and staff — to meet financial expectations and deliver standout consumer experiences rather than getting distracted by agent demands.

The goals of executives and managers center on consistently improving the quality and effectiveness of their management and leadership. They guide every company project they undertake.

Management and agent attitudes generally reflect their organizations' behaviors. Therefore, executives and managers must diligently ensure that everyone in the organization — specifically agents — work with the best interests of the company's customers, investors and operating team in mind. The goal is to create a company where transparency, accountability and a systems-focused attitude predominate.

Another goal is to create an organizational mindset that stimulates staff and agents into positive attitudes and productivity, and guides the company's approach to creating outstanding customer service.

This mindset sets the tone for how staff and agents respond and interact with their brokerage, a recognition that management sets the table for their relationships. Management defines a brokerage's ethics, mindset and attitude.

Design and Activate the Change Management Process

The reengineering of business management has been a global reality for many years under many names: Total Quality Management, rightsizing, restructuring and turnarounds. The goal of these revamps is to meet the challenges created by emerging markets and transitioning older ones by adapting and sharpening the way companies do business. In today's real estate environment, a successful business management remodel requires that brokerages make a variety of fundamental changes. They include:

- Fostering a positive attitude toward change within the company. Without the thorough support of everyone in the company, change will likely not occur as few organizations have the energy and resources necessary to overcome internal resistance. Success requires two prerequisites: the creation of a shared understanding among leadership and employees that the factors driving change are unequivocally upending the status quo, and an understanding that the entire company and its team will be better off after the change.

- Developing and empowering a management team comprised of influential decision-makers within the brokerage company to guide the change.

- Designing a process for making the change. It should function as a highly collaborative system that facilitates the transition of brokerage staff, agents and leadership from the status quo to a more effective and profitable business design.

- Anticipating and managing resistance to change by using the following effective change management outline: prepare for change, manage change and reinforce the need for change.

- Clearly identifying responsible parties for each step in the change

> "The reengineering of business management has been a global reality for many years under many names."

> "To meet even the most minimal objectives and goals, someone must be in charge."

process. Each task associated with the change-management process must be assigned to specific staff members. Senior executives must set an example of absolute support for the changes. Department heads and office managers should communicate the change message to staff and agents. Staff and agents are responsible for making changes in the company's day-to-day operation and for providing timely, ongoing feedback to management.

Institute a Diligent Focus on Improving

Perfection is not possible or feasible and everything can always be improved. This understanding undergirds the concept of continuous improvement. Instilling this attitude into the organization will immediately shift company mindset away from status quo operation, which helps protect MEB firms from disruption. They continuously strive to disrupt themselves.

This thinking will erode disconnected operations and support a team-oriented approach to problem-solving and operations. This mentality requires everyday buy-in from every staff member and agent. This is a mandatory prerequisite to success in the new real estate business environment.

Use Business Metrics to Guide the Process

Metrics are the lifeblood of making critical business decisions in the MEB model. A business metric, also known as a key performance indicator (KPI), is an element of business performance that can be quantifiably measured and used to track and assess results.

Establish Best Practices and Operational Standards

The idea of mandatory companywide best practices and operational standards contradicts the legacy concept of agents as lone rangers. While this chapter does not address the issue of employee agents, it will make it abundantly clear that agents can no longer operate as freewheeling, autonomous actors. (For more on the delicate and legally involved topic of agent employment status, see 2016 Swanepoel Trends Report, "Independent Contractors — The Delicate Equilibrium.") Business leaders in other industries have long understood that management must control every aspect of a business for it to thrive in the long term. As residential real estate industry matures, that same truth is now emerging for the real estate brokerage model.

In the MEB business model, the management team exists to manage the business not the egos, demands and expectations of agents.

Establish Leadership and Best Practices

To meet even the most minimal objectives and goals, someone must be in charge. Someone must make decisions about monetization, consumer experience, and take on the associated marketing and transaction tasks. Agents are certainly capable of functioning in an organization with well-defined best practices. Nothing demonstrates these operational necessities more clearly than the rise of agent teams.

Some of the industry's highest-performing agents work on teams, many of which have well-defined operational structures. They often operate with the following basic premises: someone must be in charge; agents are capable of following established standards and procedures; and a well-managed team with best practices and operating standards can produce more together than individually.

Get Buy-In From Everyone, Especially Agents

Should each MEB design its own best practices and standards? Yes. First of all, while some industrywide standards are emerging, most efforts are sparse, not well-developed and unproven. Second, agents are a critical component to the creation of these best practices. To drive change, the company needs their buy-in.

Major companies in other industries have used the concepts outlined here for many years. These firms discovered that the best practices and standards developed by those who will be impacted by them tend to succeed better and at higher rates; they become an organic part of company culture. This is critical.

Elements of Documented Processes

Perhaps the most important element in developing best practices and operational standards is putting them down on paper and sharing them with everyone in the company. In addition to the best practices themselves, the document should include the philosophical reasons behind them. This encourages staff and agent buy-in and keeps everyone focused on the reasons for the established procedures.

It is important for brokerages to understand that nearly every activity they undertake is complex and crucial to their success. That is why documented processes are so critical and are the centerpiece of the MEB model. They make up the foundation of effective workflows, risk management and error reduction.

The majority of brokerage management and transactional procedures require more than one related documented process. When taken together, processes form a procedure, and multiple procedures make up projects. Process, procedure and projects – three of the most important words in the MEB lexicon.

Brokerage procedures define a brokerage's programs, products and services. Management is the glue that holds projects together and ensures they remain consistent with the firm's philosophy and culture. Documented processes support management in the following ways:

- Provide all levels of leadership and management with specific guidelines for their jobs and how to do them effectively.
- Cultivate accountability by establishing specific steps and identifying individuals responsible for each of them.
- Establish and sustain quality by driving consistent, measurable and predictable outcomes.
- Support efficiency by uncovering unproductive systems and actions, which can then be eliminated.
- Establish a basis from which the brokerage can continually refine and improve.
- Establish an expected structure, which brokerages can monitor and measure.
- Protect the brokerage against efforts to substitute personal preferences for documented processes.
- Provide a basis for training, coaching and accountability.

A documented process has a few key properties: It is written, easy to understand and follow, and outlines the necessary steps to complete a process or task. It can take several formats including a simple manuscript, a checklist or a more sophisticated process roadmap. As with many elements of establishing the MEB, these decisions are best made with the participation of management, staff and agents.

Steps to Creating a Documented Process

A critical element in understanding the documented process is that it is not a top-down directive from brokerage leadership. Instead, everyone involved should understand that it is a direction formed from the collaboration of all the individuals and groups who will be impacted by it. Only when all parties have vetted and provided input on the process should senior management adopt it. This exercise generally involves the following steps:

- Identify the process to be documented.
- Name the process so that it will be easy to recognize.
- List in sufficient detail the who, what, where and when of the process.
- Make sure the document sets out the "how to" in simple, concise language.
- Include a short statement about why the process is important and how it will improve brokerage workflow.
- Allow those who will be directly impacted by the process to review a draft. Then update the process based on their feedback.
- Ensure the process aligns with the company's culture and mission.
- Test out the process several times to ensure that it works, makes sense and is clearly understood.
- Communicate, train and coach those who will follow the process.
- Periodically check in with those involved in the process to make sure it is working or if it needs to be tweaked in any way.

"The time is now to take action or to be left in the dust."

Brokerages generate hundreds of business metrics. However, the majority of traditional executives and managers use them sparsely in their management process because they collect so few and analyze even fewer. Some of these traditional metrics include listing count, agent count, closings, expired listings, phone calls and empty parking spots.

While each provides perspective of the company's overall health at any particular time, they do not begin to create the overall picture that modern metrics can provide. Accordingly, a critical element of a management-by-metrics program is the collection and analysis of information related to important tasks and functions.

Choosing the important metrics to track is generally a matter of determining which support the brokerage's culture and business philosophy. Tracking these allow the management team to focus on the processes that impact the company's overall performance and how it adheres to its culture and philosophy. Each company's management-by-metrics program will differ based upon its unique culture and business philosophy. However, each organization should establish how they analyze and use the metrics they select. Below are some other important elements of a management-by-metrics program:

- Brokerages should use metrics to determine the effectiveness of their processes.

- Productivity metrics should be monitored frequently to spot and quickly respond to both positive and adverse trends.

- Monitoring metrics will provide the brokerage with the necessary knowledge to effectively direct or redirect resources.

- Over time, brokerages should use metrics to establish performance baselines they can use to determine whether new processes and innovations contribute to or detract from productivity.

- Metrics will highlight opportunities for continuous quality improvement.

In the best-managed MEBs, the analysis of metrics will lead to internal trends. These trends will help management successfully promote systems to agents, consumers and investors. Nothing speaks as clearly or as convincingly as data.

Deliver High-Impact Consumer Experience

For most of the past decade, real estate consumers have gained increased control of the homebuying and selling process thanks to vast amounts of information they have at their fingertips. This includes significant insight into and understanding of search, marketing and transaction processes.

This knowledge, coupled with expectations of quality service, has created a new brokerage challenge. Consumers make contact with a brokerage or its agents with a clear vision of what they expect. Anticipating these expectations and incorporating them into a brokeragewide consumer experience plan has become an essential task that few companies do successfully.

MEB brokerages meet this challenge by creating and delivering an extraordinary consumer experience that aligns with the company's culture and business philosophy. Best practices, operational standards and an array of documented processes back this effort up and make it sustainable.

In many ways, the design, development and implementation of a documented consumer experience lies at the heart of the MEB model. While a firm's culture and business philosophy govern why something is done, the documented processes and desired consumer experience dictate how it is done.

A great deal of research has been done on consumer experiences. Forrester Research defines consumer experience as "how customers perceive their interactions with the brokerage." The firm suggests that great a consumer experience protocol should have three components:

- It must be useful and deliver value.

- It must be easy to find and engage with its value proposition.

- It must be enjoyable and emotionally engaging.

It turns out that consumers, depending on their generation, want different things. This complicates a consumer experience blueprint and requires

> "While a firm's culture and business philosophy govern why something is done, the documented processes and desired consumer experience dictate how it is done."

brokerages to know their target customer. If 12 elements make up a universal brokerage consumer experience protocol, eight will be similar while four will differ as they address unique generational expectations (based on the brokerage's defined audience).

In delivering the perfect consumer experience, the MEB model tasks a team comprised of managers, agents, executives and consumers. However, it is important to keep in mind that the creation of the organization's official consumer experience protocol is not governed by the opinions and current practices of its agents. This is not about compromise but about identifying the consumer experience goals the entire brokerage will implement and support. The consumer experience protocol development process, as well as every process set forth in this chapter, must include an awareness of related offerings by competitors. The consumer experience protocol is a living process that brokerages will constantly need to improve as they monitor its performance. A successful protocol enables brokerages to measure, validate and improve consumer experience on an ongoing basis. This requires effective, accurate measurement and audit processes from the beginning. Such as:

- Listing each step of a client's journey to a successful transaction.

- Identifying the factors in each step that could add or detract to a quality experience.

- Identifying the distinct ways the brokerage – its brand, agents, staff and leadership –provides service to consumers. Create a documented process for each of those consumer experience touch points so the brokerage can monitor them and incorporate them into marketing and promotions.

- Communicating, training and coaching impacted teams on the established customer experience process.

- Monitoring, measuring, analyzing, continuously improving and supporting the consumer experience protocol.

"A successful protocol enables brokerages to measure, validate and improve consumer experience on an ongoing basis."

Develop Focused Financial Expectations

Another key element of the MEB model is the design, development and implementation of documented financial expectations.

First, brokerages must bake these financial expectations into their culture, business philosophy and documented processes to ensure that all elements support the company maximizing its long-term profits. While this suggestion

> "Metrics are the lifeblood of making critical business decisions."

may appear basic, few traditional brokerages actually articulate profit as a mandatory requirement in their business design. In many cases, it is assumed but not documented clearly.

A brokerage's consumer experience protocols and financial expectations should closely align. Brokerages should focus on those consumer elements that contribute to profitability.

Company financial success depends upon a brokerage's ability to generate revenues and profits from as many programs, products and services as possible. This objective demands that financial and sales best practices ensure that: every profit opportunity is exploited; events that could lead to financial risk and loss are avoided; the company optimizes profitability for existing programs, products and services; and the company constantly searches for new ways to generate profit.

Designing a consumer experience starts with the following:

- Assigning the financial design task to a team of managers, agents, executives and financial professionals.

- Identifying each program, product and service the brokerage believes it can generate profits from. Determine which programs, products and services make a profit, determine their viability, and identify the factors that add or detract from their value.

- Creating a document that identifies how to maximize marketing success of each product or service.

- Communicating, training and coaching impacted teams on the brokerage's financial expectations, and then monitor, measure analyze, continuously improve and sustain them.

Systematize Administrative and Transaction Documentation

A viable, thriving MEB requires streamlined management, administration and transaction documentation. This is a weak link in many traditional brokerages and therefore worthy of focus. It is important because:

- These activities significantly contribute to a well-organized work environment and a sense of individual responsibility, accountability and commitment.

- These assets enhance morale, administrative discipline and productivity by improving communication and ensuring that variations to documented processes are transparent.

- Management and administrative excellence reduce wasted time and unproductive behavior. More effective communication leads to increased transparency, which further improves communication, trust and efficiency.

- The Management-Empowered Brokerage must use its standardization and administrative documented process system in every part of the business where transparency, accountability and responsibility can contribute to success and profitability.

- The management and administrative standardization system must be supported at every level of management and supervision. Every executive, manager, staff member and agent must be responsible and accountable for using the system. Failure to do so must have consequences.

- The ultimate goal is a documented orderly and efficient administrative and transaction system capable of supporting the business.

The following tasks are critical in the design, development and implementation of the system. They include:

- Collecting and closely examining all documentation and processes currently used.

- Determining which documents and processes are essential to administrative and transactional excellence.

- Reviewing, amending, publishing and cataloging all essential documentation into common formats and convert to a PDF to facilitate use and organization.

- Implementing appropriateness, management review and approval of all proposed documentation at every personnel level within the organization.

- Creating documented processes with standards and best practices for each transactional element.

- Integrating the documented processes into the organization's management and operational software and technology.

- Ensuring the completed system processes are subject to continuous improvement through ongoing quality review and periodic audits.

Takeaway

Over the past several years, real estate industry thoughtleaders have uncovered a wide range of brokerage model trends, opportunities and disruptions. For the most part, the industry treated these insights with disdain or denial, declaring that these challenges were nothing more than fads. Yet these transformational forces are leaving bigger and bigger marks on the industry. The time is now to take action or be left in the dust as industry winners evolve into mature, well-designed businesses.

In 2017, a wide range of new forces have worked their way into all facets of the mainstream real estate industry. Given their number and influence, the industry has reached a point of no return. Brokerages need to evolve their business models to meet the new realities overwhelmingly shaping the industry.

These new models need to be nimble so that brokerages can continue to adapt, evolve and take advantage of the changes in the industry. The revolution in real estate transactions, lead generation and consumer experience and expectations are sure to continue.

The MEB model describes the new brokerage business model of the next decade. We have not seen it implemented at scale in real estate. This chapter is intended to give readers details of its proposed design, enabling them to take action and implement their own transformation to the modern real estate economy. More importantly, we made it flexible enough for any brokerage, large or small, to take this critical step.

This outline offers firms an opportunity to shift their organization's focus from the individual to the strength of a team. It provides a path for brokerages to address the shortcomings of the traditional model by leveraging a set of universal business best practices and standards. It provides a roadmap that incorporates brokerages' histories while also helping them successfully address current challenges and opportunities.

The T3 Sixty team has spent the past two decades studying the events and trends that have come together to create this moment. Take note, and take advantage.

Congratulations!

The most powerful people
in residential real estate for
2017/2018.

01
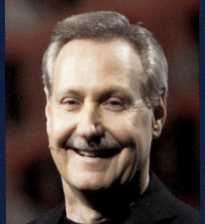
Gary Keller
Co-Founder, Chairman
Keller Williams

02

Spencer Rascoff
CEO
Zillow Group

03
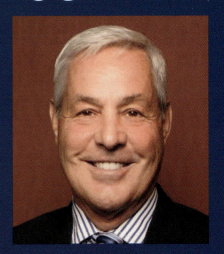
Ron Peltier
Chairman and CEO
HomeServices of America

04

Dave Liniger
Co-Founder, Chairman and CEO
Re/Max

05

Ryan M. Schneider
President and CEO
Realogy Holdings

06

Bruce Zipf
President and CEO
NRT

07

John Davis
CEO
Keller Williams

08

Robert "Bob" Goldberg
CEO
National Association of Realtors

09

Glenn Kelman
President and CEO
Redfin

10

Ryan O'Hara
President and CEO
Move, Inc.

11

Amy Bohutinsky
COO
Zillow Group

12

Howard "Hoddy" Hanna & Helen Hanna Casey
Chairman & CEO
Hanna Holdings

13

John Peyton
President and CEO
Realogy Franchise Group

14
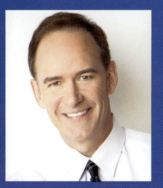
Philip "Phil" Soper
President and CEO
Brookfield Real Estate Services

15

Charlie Young
President and CEO
Coldwell Banker

See the entire list at sp200.com

03

Rise of the Modern Discount Brokerage

A Model for the Digital Era

A new generation of discount brokerage firms with well-honed operations, investor funding, and big plans to scale their businesses nationally are gaining traction in the real estate industry. They do not offer lower fees because they provide stripped-down service, but, rather, by leveraging technology and systems to lower costs, they provide full-spectrum brokerage services to consumers for fees below traditional rates. These upstart Modern Discount Brokerages are gaining market share in real estate's modern era. Here is what you need to know.

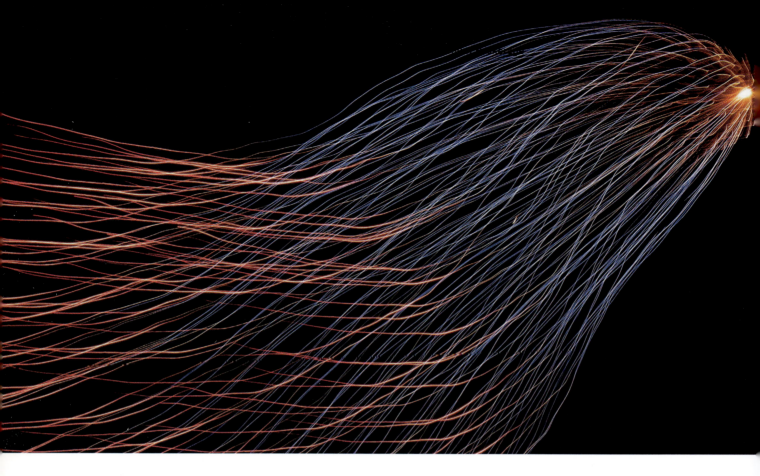

Modern Discount Brokerages

Discount brokerage models have been around for decades; many focused on helping for-sale-by-owners (FSBOs) list their home on MLSs and provide other core marketing services such as flyers and yard signs. Help-U-Sell (helpusell.com), a discount brokerage franchise system founded in 1976, grew into a national brand with this model. These discount brokerages have experienced ups and downs over the years as seller's markets — in which frothy buyer demand makes selling homes at market rate easier to do without an agent's personal attention, marketing and connections — have swung to buyer's markets where selling at top dollar requires more skill and effort.

However, a new breed of discount brokerage built on technology and a companywide systemized approach to real estate is emerging that pairs low fees with increasingly robust services that we call the Modern Discount Brokerage (MDB). Digital marketing, automated and measurable advertising strategies, technology-enabled economies of scale, and real estate team-like agent services fuel the rise of this new digital-enabled model.

These firms are different from their low-fee predecessors. One of the primary differentiators is the vast advancement in technology over the last decade that has fundamentally reshaped the way real estate businesses market their services, communicate internally and with prospects, organize and optimize followup and more. Many brokerage firms are taking advantage of these advancements – the difference between them and MDBs is that MDBs built

> "A new breed of discount brokerage built on technology and a companywide systemized approach to real estate is emerging."

their businesses from the ground up with these technologies. They are built for the Amazon, Uber, Airbnb era. They have models that can profitably scale lockstep with technology — they can profitably win with every tech-borne efficiency. Firms not built in the digital era often must reverse-engineer their models and systems to leverage the power the digital era unleashes.

Even though they charge flat fees or commissions below traditional rates, MDBs offer consumers comprehensive, contract-to-close services. Many of them offer in-home consultations, professional photos and videos, lockboxes, yard signs, MLS listings, showing services, contract negotiation, closing coordination — many of the services provided by traditional, full-fee brokerages and agents. One of the most prominent MDBs is Redfin (redfin.com), which operates in over 80 markets, went public in July 2017 and had a valuation of over $1.8 billion in November 2017. Others include U.K.-based Purplebricks (purplebricks.com), which expanded to the U.S. in September 2017 after explosive growth in its home country, and Denver-based Redefy Real Estate (redefy.com), which has quadrupled its sales volume in the last three years.

> "These newer firms are built from the ground up to scale, feature streamlined company and agent operations, and use technology to drive down traditional brokerage costs."

While they offer similar services, MDBs do things differently than traditional real estate companies. They essentially run as well-oiled real estate agent teams, with centralized services, custom in-house technology and well-honed, streamlined systems. Their agents often specialize in specific tasks that foster proficiency, speed and quality and create an efficiency flywheel effect.

The emergence of these models accompanies the changing role of agents in the industry. As we chronicled in the No. 1 Trend in the 2017 Swanepoel Trends Report, "The Hypergrowth of Teams," more agents are working on teams as specialists than as everything-under-the-sun generalists. MDBs expand this trend into the brokerage model. The same technology, operations and consumer expectations that fuel the rise of real estate agent teams underpin these models. MDBs silo their agents' duties into component parts, often with a mix of employee, independent contractor agents and centralized support staff. For example, one team member handles inbound leads while others meet consumers and focus on closings, another manages the transaction and negotiation and another shepherds a deal to close.

Staples of Emerging Brokerage Models

- Well-honed centralized operations.
- Mix of employee agents and independent contractor agents.
- Assembly-line approach to service with agents filling well-defined roles.
- Sophisticated digital marketing.
- Brokerage-led marketing and customer acquisition.
- Flat fees to consumers.
- Virtual tour technology.
- Consumer-focused models.
- Technology and models built with a vision to double-end deals.
- Business models built for higher volumes of transactions.
- Businesses and operations designed to scale.

MDBs are designed to scale with streamlined operations, systems and technology baked into the core of their model. Their design also reflects the evolution of consumer expectations and self-serve habits molded by cutting-edge e-commerce, on-demand service and digitally-mediated trust from companies such as Amazon, Uber and Airbnb.

The pitch these firms make to consumers does not overly focus on discounted rates and lower or stripped-down service. In many cases, their marketing centers on a better experience and great service, in addition to lower fees. Traditional brokers and agents may find it difficult to compete against this new model if it takes hold across the country.

Technology and Outside Investors Spurring the Trend

The digital revolution undergirds the rise of MDBs. The increased access to data and transparency provided by sites such as Zillow — which widely publishes information on nearly every home in the U.S. that would shock 2005 homebuyers and sellers — has made it easier, and cheaper, for brokerages and agents to serve homebuyers and sellers. The ability to easily run targeted marketing campaigns through Facebook and other platforms has changed customer-acquisition strategies. Technology has increased transparency, the ability to streamline operations, operate more efficiently as remote teams and more effectively centralize operations, all which reduce operating costs.

The ability to expose a listing to millions of homebuyers on Zillow with the click of a button has also made it cheaper and easier for brokerages and agents to market listings.

Technology's impact on real estate transactions cannot be overstated. A change in how homebuyers find their home illustrates one way it has impacted transactions. A majority of buyers now find the home they purchase themselves. After growing steadily over the last two decades, the percentage of buyers who found the home they purchased themselves on the internet surpassed 50 percent for the first time in 2016, trumping the percentage that found homes through their agent (34 percent), according to NAR's 2016 Profile of Home Buyers and Sellers. In 2001, those numbers were 8 percent and 48 percent, respectively.

Outside investors are also helping drive this trend. Fueled by venture capital funding, five MDBs have launched in the last 24 months. For more on how outside investors are shaping real estate, see Trend No. 1, "Follow the Money."

> "An MDB is, in many regards, a rethought brokerage."

Modern Discount Brokerages (MDB)

MDB, URL and Year Founded	Markets Served	Total VC Funding Through Nov 2017	Projected 2017 Production
Door Inc. (doorhomes.com) 2015	Dallas and Austin, Texas	$3.1 Million	270 Units
Faira (faira.com) 2015	Washington State	$3.0 Million	N/A
Homie (homie.com) 2015	Utah	$8.3 Million	800-Plus Units
Houwzer (houwzer.com) 2015	Philadelphia and Washington, D.C.	$2.0 Million	350 Units
Purplebricks (purplebricks.com) 2014	U.K., Australia and Southern California	$88.2 Million[1]	N/A
Reali (reali.com) 2015	San Francisco Bay Area, Sacramento and Solano Counties in California	$10.0 Million	N/A
Redefy Real Estate (redefy.com) 2013	Denver; Northern Colorado; Colorado Springs, Colorado; Tampa, Florida; Phoenix; and Greenville, South Carolina.[2]	Undisclosed	Over 1,500 Units[2]
Redfin (redfin.com) 2004	All 50 U.S. States, 84 Markets	$167 Million	Over 26,000 Units
Trelora (trelora.com) 2011	Denver	$5.1 Million	Over 1,200 Units

[1] Pre-IPO funding.
[2] Company-owned offices as of September 2017.

Source: T3 Sixty using Crunchbase data, Door Homes, Homie, Houwzer, Trelora and Redfin's financial statements, Redefy Real Estate.

The Players

As these emerging MDB models gain market share and consumer awareness, their widespread acceptance could significantly contribute to the compression of real estate commission rates across the industry or split the market into two tiers: high-touch, full-service, full commission, agent-led brokerage models at one level; low-cost, system-led MDB models on another. Brokerages who do not offer standout service or a strong local brand might not be able to compete with MDBs who offer comparable service at much lower costs. As Redfin, Purplebricks and others profiled in this report gain market share, they leave an increasing number of satisfied consumers familiar with their model in their wake. This social proof could spur exponential growth.

Redfin

Redfin's profile is burning bright following its July 28, 2017, IPO, which raised $138 million for the firm. From 2014 to 2016, the brokerage roughly doubled its annual transaction side count and annual sales volume to 25,868 and $16.2 billion, respectively. The firm lost double-digit millions each of those three years, but losses declined as a percentage of overall revenue from 19.7 percent in 2014 to 8.4 percent in 2016. In the third quarter 2017, the firm reported a $10.6 million profit on $109 million in revenue.

Redfin Overview

Timeline	Founded in 2004, launched in 2006, expanded nationally in 2015, went public on July 28, 2017.
Model	Uses employee agents, paid in part based on customer satisfaction, to serve consumers it attracts through its powerful real estate search platform.
Commission/Fees	Listing fee of 1.5 percent; 1 percent in over 20 markets. Provides a rebate to buyers, which averaged $3,500 in 2016.
Markets	All 50 states, 84 markets.

The company charges sellers a commission of 1.5 percent in most of its markets; it lowered this fee to 1 percent in over 20 markets in fall 2017 after testing it in a few markets earlier in the year. It has market-dependent minimum fees, which range from approximately $3,000 to $5,500, encourages sellers to offer market-rate commissions to buyer's agents, and provides buyers a rebate, which averaged $3,500 in 2016.

Redfin Statistics

Year	Units Closed[1] (YoY Growth)	Sales Volume (YoY Growth)	Agent Count[2] (YoY Growth)
2014	12,688	$8.4B	422
2015	18,586 (+46%)	$12.3B (+46%)	591 (+40%)
2016	25,868 (+39%)	$16.2B (+32%)	736 (+29%)

Source: Redfin S-1 Filing
[1] Closed by Refin's in-house agents.
[2] Lead agents interact with Redfin customers and are supported by other Redfin staff and agents.

Redfin promises clients robust service. Sellers receive an in-home consultation, professional photography, 3D virtual tour, home showings, yard sign, open houses and more. Buyers also receive traditional levels of service.

The company has salaried agents, whose base pay accounted for just 27 percent of total compensation in 2016. Much of their pay is based on the results of customer satisfaction surveys and a percentage of the sales price of the homes they help sell.

Redfin has had a discount design since its inception in 2004 and established providing value to consumers as a founding mission. It focuses on this by balancing service with price, making a bet that the brokerage that provides consumers better value will win. The Seattle-based firm began representing buyers and sellers in Seattle and the San Francisco Bay Area in 2006 with a reduced listing commission rate and buyer rebates. As it expanded over the years, sometimes it launched in markets as a referral engine before bringing on local in-house agents.

Redfin's seller and buyer rebates are not set in stone, according to CEO Glenn Kelman. The firm can increase or decrease them to adapt to the market. In seller's markets, for example, Redfin can dial up its seller discount and shrink its buyer rebates; when the market shifts, it can decrease the seller rebate and increase the buyer rebate. In this way, it hopes to adapt, and survive, shifting markets.

The company has seen the most success in bigger metropolitan areas with higher price points but, as its business scales and operations become more efficient, Kelman says the price floor of homes it can profitably service will sink lower and lower. It once did not make a profit when representing buyers on a $350,000 home; now it easily does, he points out.

As technology, diligent measurement, process refinement and scale increases, the firm notes efficiencies, profits and market opportunity will increase and costs lower with economies of scale as it grows. The brokerage side of

> "Seller and buyer rebates are not set in stone."

its operations are profitable, according to Kelman; now the firm just needs to do enough production to overcome its overhead costs, particularly those of software development and engineers.

Technology

Redfin marries technology with service in an aim to deliver the value at the heart of its mission. As CEO Kelman says, "Without technology, this wouldn't work." It uses data from its in-house technology platform to constantly test and refine its operations. Read more about its platform in Trend No. 8 in the 2017 Swanepoel Trends Report, "The Brokerage Platform Battle."

Superior technology lowers customer acquisitions costs, facilitates automation and increases speed, which boosts conversion rates. As a result, Redfin is optimizing its technology for service speed and quality with the goal of winning more deals and clients. The firm's 2016 production of 26,000 units with 763 lead agents illustrates its model's efficiency (Redfin also has support agents, but maintains a far fewer amount than lead agents). A traditional firm would need approximately four times as many agents to close the same number of transaction sides.

The firm's proprietary technology platform streamlines company operations, makes agents more efficient, and offers the capability to measure, track and test extensively. It also helps consumers search for homes, keep track of the market, estimate home values and request showings. Redfin's real estate search site and mobile app are among the nation's most popular with consumers, in company with industry leaders Zillow, realtor.com and Trulia.

Most Popular Real Estate Sites in October 2017

Traffic Rank	Site	Unique Visitors[1]
1	zillow.com	23.3 Million
2	realtor.com	11.5 Million
3	trulia.com	9.1 Million
4	redfin.com	5.0 Million

Source: Hitwise division of Connexity
[1] Includes both desktop and mobile traffic, but not mobile app traffic.
For information on traffic reporting see notes on page 75.

Redfin's marketing philosophy centers on building top-notch real estate consumer technology instead of investing millions in advertising. The company aims to lower customer acquisition costs further by increasing the percentage of site visitors who are serious buyers and sellers. Responding to inquiries and meeting with consumers who are not close to transacting detracts from the benefit of having a popular website and potentially burdens it with additional work that does not generate revenue.

Redfin uses machine learning algorithms to refine consumer listing recommendations, Redfin Estimate, its automated valuation model, and Redfin Hot Homes, a tool that alerts consumers to the listings big data suggests are likely to sell soon. The firm also streamlines operations with automation, including tour-scheduling. For example, the company's mobile-optimized agent tools automatically suggest listings for agents to recommend to clients and provides related email templates to make it easier and quicker for them to send recommendations.

Having a proprietary technology platform also provides data that enhances training and effective best practices. For example, Redfin knows that if a buyer waives offer contingencies, the chance of selling the home more than doubles – clear data powers that insight, not a hunch. A powerful in-house technology platform provides Redfin the opportunity to add new features as technology and consumer expectations evolve – it is built to adapt and scale with the digital era.

While these tools make the company more efficient, it has not been profitable for much of its existence. As the company grows and handles larger volumes, it believes economies of scale and a positive feedback loop will support profitability.

Agents
Redfin organizes its agents into two classes: lead agents and support agents. Lead agents are primarily responsible for working closely with clients and supporting them through each step of a transaction; licensed, desk-bound support agents take calls, fill in gaps and respond quickly to all inquiries. The company has transaction coordinators who help facilitate the closing and works to automate the administrative tasks all employees face.

All Redfin agents are employees, which allows it to better train and hold them accountable for delivering a higher level of service. As of Sept. 30, 2017, Redfin had 1,028 lead agents, just under half of its total employee count of 2,229 at that time. Most employees work either as support agents, managers or administrative staff in its approximately 50 offices across the U.S.

Like most brokerages, having high-quality agents is critical to the firm's model and Kelman says it spends significant time and resources on training. Redfin recruits and trains its agents to be well-rounded service providers. As with traditional models, the company wants agents to form deep, meaningful relationships with clients to increase their satisfaction and drive repeat and referral business.

Ancillary Services
Redfin launched its mortgage and title businesses in 2016 and 2017, respectively, as part of an effort to provide an efficient, fast end-to-end experience for consumers and to generate additional revenue. In 2016, 46 percent of its buyer clients used its title and settlement service in the eight states it was available.

Purplebricks

Launched by two former U.K. real estate agents in 2014, Purplebricks has taken its home market by storm with a technology-focused discount brokerage model aided by large marketing spends and local agent representation. Instead of the typical 1.5 percent listing commission U.K. agents charge (buyer agency does not exist in the U.K.), Purplebricks lists and markets homes for a flat fee of approximately $1,148. Based on the average U.K. home sales price of $299,464 in July 2017, this represents savings of $3,344, or 74 percent, compared to a 1.5 percent traditional commission rate.

Purplebricks Overview

Timeline	Founded in 2012, launched in 2014, went public in December 2015, expanded to Australia in August 2016 and California in September 2017.
Model	Purplebricks delivers leads to in-house independent contractor agents who work in exclusive ZIP code territories. Buyers, sellers and agents have access to a dashboard that streamlines communication and encourages consumers to participate in finding their own home, making offers, negotiating prices and showing and viewing homes.
Commission/ Fees	Sellers pay $3,200 regardless of a sale. Buyers receive a $1,000 rebate upon closing.
Markets	U.S. (only California as of October 2017), U.K., Australia

In fiscal year 2017, Purplebricks, which has no brick-and-mortar offices, represented sellers on approximately 40,000 sales. This was roughly double fiscal year 2016's amount and eight times its first-year total. This total represented 3.3 percent of the U.K. market, according to analysts at financial services firm UBS in March 2017.

Purplebricks UK Statistics

Year	Units Closed[1] (YoY Growth)	Sales Volume (YoY Growth)	# of Agents[2] (YoY Growth)
2014 (launch year)	4,843	$1.13 billion/£832 million	79
2015	20,644 (+326%)	$3.75 billion/£2.77 billion (+232%)	205 (+159%)
2016	41,739 (+102%)	$7.84 billion/£5.8 billion (+109%)	448 (+119%)

Source: Purplebricks annual investor presentations for 2015, 2016 and 2017.
[1] Fiscal year ended March 31 in respective years.
[2] Estimated by dividing annual revenue by average revenue per transaction.

Three years in, the company is on a rapid growth track. It went public on the London Stock Exchange in December 2015, expanded to Australia in August 2016, and the U.S. in September 2017. In October 2017 its market cap was over $1.3 billion, more than triple that of its public U.K. brokerage rivals Countrywide (countrywide.co.uk), Foxtons Group (foxtonsgroup.co.uk) and

LSL Property Services (lslps.co.uk), whose market caps were $358 million, $238 million, and $319 million, respectively, at that time.

Purplebricks expanded to Australia in August 2016. In its first eight months in the country, it grew to 77 agents, did over $430 million in sales and generated $4.6 million in revenue. The firm raised $62 million through a special stock offering in early 2017 to bring its low-fee, technology-aided brokerage model to the U.S. It opened shop in Los Angeles in September with plans to expand throughout California before launching nationwide.

The firm adapted its model to fit the U.S. buyer agency model while maintaining the pillars that anchor its U.K. success: a technology platform that facilitates both buyer and seller self-service, local independent contractor agent representation, significant brand marketing, no brokerage offices and flat seller fees.

In the Los Angeles area, Purplebricks lists homes for a flat fee of $3,200, which the seller pays regardless of whether the home sells (sellers can defer payment for up to six months if the home does not sell). The firm offers market-rate buy-side commissions to buyer agents on its listings and rebates $1,000 of the buy-side commission to its buyers upon close.

The company chose Los Angeles as its launch city for its dense population, which makes its intensive local brand marketing more effective, and its high average sale price, which makes its low-fee pitch more appealing to sellers, according to Purplebricks U.S. CEO Eric Eckardt.

Sellers receive an in-house consultation, local agent support (with access to 24/7 agent support as backup), a Matterport 3D virtual tour, professional photography, a yard sign and a lockbox among other traditional services. Homeowners can request a Purplebricks agent to show their homes, but the company makes it easy to schedule self-showings through its dashboard.

Technology
Purplebricks serves clients with licensed in-house agents, and supplements them with a technology platform built to encourage clients to perform some activities themselves such as negotiating directly with the buyer or seller (or their respective agent), submitting offers, approving and requesting showings, listing a property and accessing offers in real time as a seller.

Agents
Purplebricks uses a mix of salaried and independent contractor agents. A centralized team of salaried agents works in an office, operating as inside sales agents qualifying inbound leads and routing them to the company's independent contractor agents, which the firm calls Local Real Estate Experts. Salaried agents also respond to consumer inquiries and field questions from clients who are unable to reach their local agent, whether because they are

calling after-hours (in-house agents are available 24/7) or the agent is busy with another client.

In the U.S., Purplebricks' Local Real Estate Experts have exclusive ZIP code territories in which they live and where no other Purplebricks agent may take a listing. Purplebricks pays them a flat fee for each listing they secure. On the buy side, agents pay 40 percent of the commission to Purplebricks. Lead agents in a territory can build teams as local demand grows, just as Purplebricks agents do in the U.K. In these cases, lead agents earn a split of their team members' earnings. Once a home sale contract is signed, the lead agent no longer interacts with the client as transaction coordinators in the in-house closing division take over.

Marketing

Unlike Redfin, Purplebricks has an aggressive brand marketing strategy. Part of its pitch to Los Angeles agents in fall 2017 included a promise to spend nearly $2 million per month on TV and radio campaigns. In its first U.S. video ad, the company introduces "real misery" as "the misery you feel when you pay too much in commission and get nothing more for your money."

Redfy Real Estate

Launched in 2013 by former Keller Williams Realty real estate agent Jordan Connett and real estate investor Chris Rediger, Redefy Real Estate offers sellers a simple proposition: Sell your home for a flat fee of $3,000 (it charges sellers a 1 percent commission for homes over $1 million). The company also works with buyers at traditional commission rates.

Redefy Overview

Timeline	Founded in 2011, launched in January 2013 and started franchising in January 2014.
Model	Licensed as a brokerage with in-house and independent contractor agents. Has company-owned and franchised offices.
Commission/ Fees	Sellers pay a flat fee of $3,000. Homes over $1 million carry a 1 percent commission. It does not provide buyer rebates.
Markets	15 markets, 12 states (as of September 2017)

The Denver-based brokerage uses in-house technology, a mix of employee and independent contractor agents, and a refined process to create

Why Canada's Largest Real Estate Company Bought an MDB

Canadian real estate giant Brookfield Real Estate Services (brookfieldresinc.com), which has over 300 franchisees, 689 offices and more than 18,000 agents at its franchised and company-owned offices, purchased the Quebec-based, 700-agent Proprio Direct (proprio-direct.com) in June 2017 to participate in the growing trend of alternative brokerage models.

While Proprio Direct has centralized operations and expects sellers to hold their own open houses, it differs in some ways from the MDB models profiled in this chapter. It targets FSBO sellers, which make up a larger percentage of the market in Quebec than in the U.S., up to 30 percent by some estimates. Its offering focuses on technology and the benefit of helping sellers find their own buyer, allowing them to save on the buy-side commission. However, it charges sellers a traditional commission, and, as Brookfield President and CEO Phil Soper points out, many sellers end up offering buyer's agents a traditional rate. Sellers with little to no training and perhaps a full-time job may find it difficult to locate a buyer.

Proprio Direct has 31 staff to support its 700 agents. Compare that 23-to-1 agent-to-staff ratio to the 10-to-1 ratio at traditional brokerages in Brookfield's portfolio. The MDB has no brick-and-mortar offices, has all digital systems, has cloud-based training and coaching, and has a sophisticated online lead-gen system with a centralized call center that scrubs inbound leads and transfers them to agents (at a 50-50 split). "It's a rethought brokerage," Soper says. It is also the most profitable brokerage in Brookfield's portfolio, he adds. Brookfield worries about the sustainability of traditional brokerages in smaller markets as they increasingly struggle to achieve profitability.

"We've been interested in the low-fee, narrow service market for a while," Soper says. Proprio Direct presented an opportunity for the company to jump in with two feet.

efficiencies that support its low-fee model. As with other MDBs, its model is based on a vision that technology can deliver efficiency and cost-savings that translate to lower consumer fees. The approach is bearing fruit: From 2014 to 2016, Redefy grew its transaction sides and sales volume fourfold.

Redefy Real Estate Statistics

Year	Units Closed (YoY Growth)	Sales Volume (YoY Growth)
2014	325	$154.9 million
2015	1,086 (+234%)	$321.5 million (+108%)
2016	1,866 (+72%)	$598.5 million (+86%)

Source: Redefy Real Estate

Unlike Redfin and Purplebricks, Redefy operates a franchise wing in addition to its company-owned offices. It had 12 company-owned offices and five franchisees supported by 13 salaried agents and 115 independent contractor agents in 12 states as of September 2017.

The company provides sellers full service for its relatively low flat fee. For the $3,000 listing fee, sellers receive an in-home consultation, professional photography, yard signs, lockboxes, showings, and negotiation and transaction support. Buyers, who pay traditional commission rates, receive traditional full-service support.

Technology

Redefy uses in-house technology to streamline its operations and lower costs. Its CRM powers everything its agents do, merging transaction management, email marketing, lead-tracking and more into one system. The platform automatically alerts parties when their attention is needed as a transaction moves down the track to close. For more on the next era of CRMs, see Trend No. 8, "Smart CRMs Go Mainstream."

This creates efficiencies. For example, Redefy scrubs all leads through a centralized in-house call center. Employees route qualified leads to a general manager of the region where the lead is looking to transact; the general manager then directs the lead to the appropriate agent. That process takes about 30 seconds, according to Rediger. A portion of call center employees are also licensed agents, which means they can set a listing appointment or take a listing if on the phone with a hot lead.

In late 2017, the firm began testing a platform that allows consumers to list their home themselves with agent oversight. From a dashboard, sellers will be able to change MLS info, including descriptions and photos, view and sign all documents, chat live with an agent, request home showings and more. The company believes this will expand its market to homes farther from its service centers where it might not be cost-effective to provide discount services with in-person agent visits and consultations. Instead, agents can provide guidance over the phone to these sellers and list the home without in-house visits, which can be cost-prohibitive given the long drive times visiting these sellers would involve.

Agents

Redefy independent contractor agents, also called "field" agents, earn a flat fee of $200 when they secure a listing and $300 when it closes. On buy-side deals they collect a traditional listing commission, which they split with the brokerage 50-50 if the client came through Redefy or 80-20 if they found the buyer themselves.

Once field agents secure a listing, one of the firm's 30 salaried "contract manager" agents takes over. The listing enters the company's system with tight broker control because the agents handling these operations are W-2 employees. Since they are licensed in multiple states, contract managers can help facilitate deals remotely, including across state lines. This gives the firm flexibility as it can shift resources to different markets as activity fluctuates among them.

Because Redefy is so process-oriented, the model only works when agents diligently follow the system, Redefy co-founder Chris Rediger says. As a result, agents newer to real estate tend to thrive while experienced agents used to their own workflow tend to buck the system. Redefy's systems and training ensure they provide acceptable levels of service. As specialized service providers, Redefy agents do not need to manage a website, think about SEO or pay for marketing; they just respond to the leads Redefy delivers.

Marketing

Redefy relies heavily on digital marketing to generate leads. It does not brand individual agents, choosing to market the company and model instead. The firm has an inbound marketing philosophy and does not make cold calls. Instead it chooses to focus on advertising and content that entices sellers to reach out for more information. When they do, the company's in-house call center scrubs the leads and distributes them to agents.

Redefy monitors its costs per lead closely and manages its marketing to that metric. Marketing is one of the key factors that will determine the firm's growth, according to Rediger. Introducing the newer model to consumers and getting them to trust it enough to give it a try is an uphill battle.

Emerging MDBs

To provide deeper perspective on this trend, T3 Sixty researched several emerging MDB players in addition to the larger players profiled at length in the chapter. These are among a handful of MDBs who have received funding recently and are building businesses in markets across the U.S.

Door Inc.

Founded in 2015, Dallas-based Door Inc. closed 100 transactions in 2016 and was on track to do 270 units in 2017 in September, according to CEO Alex Doubet. The firm charges buyers and sellers a flat fee of $5,000. Eighteen of its 20 employees are licensed real estate agents; all are W-2 employees and fill specific agent roles. The firm provides full service to both buyers and sellers, producing 3-D virtual tours, marketing and negotiating final price for sellers (but does not hold open houses) and showing homes, writing offers, negotiating price and handling paperwork for buyers. The firm expanded to Austin, Texas, in late 2017.

Door Homes CEO and Founder Alex Doubet:
"The world has changed. In 2016, a majority of homebuyers bought a home they found themselves. Door Homes is a next-generation residential real estate transaction platform. Put simply, our goal is to use technology and improved operating capabilities to deliver a better experience across the residential value chain for a better price. Clients enjoy a technology platform that provides clear visibility into where the transaction stands, a specialized and professional agent to guide them through the process, at a fantastic price. All of this for a $5,000 fixed fee."

Homie

Before founding Homie in 2015, Johnny Hanna ran multifamily real estate software giant Entrata (entrata.com) as co-president. Homie, which did approximately 800 units in 2017 through September, has 60 employees, 20 of which are agents all of whom are W-2 employees. The firm provides less service to buyers and sellers than other MDBs in this chapter. Sellers show and stage their own homes and take the lead on negotiations; Homie encourages buyers to reach out to listing agents to tour homes they are interested in. Sellers pay $1,498 in two installments; buyers receive up to $5,000 as a rebate. The firm focuses on developing and automating as many processes as it can.

Homie CEO Johnny Hanna:
"Homie aims to automate the entire process of buying and selling a home. We are the perfect combination of human touch and technology, helping homeowners sell their home for top dollar, quickly, for a low flat fee. Homie also assists buyers, offering a rebate of thousands of dollars at close. We are a team of licensed agents, lawyers and technologists who assist our clients from first contact to close, while helping them save thousands of dollars along the way."

Houwzer

Houwzer (houwzer.com) provides full service to sellers for a flat fee of $495 and full service to buyers at traditional commission rates. Launched in early 2015, the firm aims to capture buy-side business and referrals at traditional commission rates to power its low-fee listing model, which includes full service: unlimited showings, social media and email marketing, professional photo and video and a technology-driven workflow. The company is gaining traction. Between 2015 and 2017 it increased annual units sevenfold and sales volume fivefold. In May 2017, it raised $2 million in seed funding and plans to make its first foray out of Philadelphia in early 2018 when it expects to launch operations in Washington, D.C. Houwzer had 50 full-time employees as of September 2017, 30 of which were W-2 employee real estate agents. Houwzer agents and staff have specialized roles including dedicated listing agents (by area), buyer agents, inside sales agents (outside of office hours the firm uses a chatbot), buyer admins and listing admins.

Houwzer CEO and Founder Mike Maher:
"Houwzer's mission is to reimagine every aspect of the home buying and selling experience by providing savvy homeowners the most exceptional service at the fairest price – simultaneously reducing the time, cost, and friction of homeownership. The traditional relationships between the broker, the agent and the customer are broken. Houwzer has rebuilt those relationships in a way that optimizes the outcomes for all parties. Coupled with world-class employee satisfaction ratings, Houwzer's customer net promoter score is 91, higher than USAA and Apple. As we expand our coverage areas and offerings, it is clear we are the most competitively priced, full-service brokerage on the planet."

Trelora

For a flat fee of $2,500, Denver-based Trelora provides sellers professional photography, showing services, negotiation services, a yard sign and lockbox. For the same fee, it also offers buyers traditional levels of service including in-person home tours, writing offers and providing transaction guidance through closing. The firm has developed its own CRM that records all communications agents perform, including phone calls; it makes these communication records available to clients. Of the firm's 36 employees, 12 are software engineers and 12 are salaried, licensed agents. Like other MDBs, every brokerage role in the company has been narrowed and focused. For example, the firm's four listing agents just visit homes and suggest prices; they do hundreds of listing appointments each year. The firm expects to do over 1,200 sides in 2017, according to CEO Joshua Hunt.

Trelora CEO and Founder Joshua Hunt:
"Trelora has a mission to create a best-in-class, full-service real estate experience for a fraction of the cost of traditional Realtors. That is why Trelora is the word Realtor jumbled up. Trelora agents close over 200 deals each year, making them among the most productive nationwide. Our customer service is second-to-none — with a customer satisfaction score more than double the industry average to prove it. Our proprietary technology platform gives our clients 24/7 access to their deal and their agent so they are always in the driver's seat. With our dedication to the client and technology, we're changing real estate for the better."

Takeaway

Huge advances in technology have made agents' jobs easier and brought consumers deeper into all aspects of a real estate transaction, from choosing homes as buyers to showing homes as sellers. These changes have fueled the proliferation of a new era of low-fee, full-service brokerage models we call Modern Discount Brokerages.

These firms offer straightforward, full-service agent representation for a fraction of traditional commission rates. They have an increasing amount of investor money to fuel and hone their models but they are not without risks: Some rely on hiring inexperienced agents, others allow clients to write their own offers or negotiate their own deals, which can lead to derailed deals and damaged reputations.

Logic suggests that MDBs will grow market share, but time will tell if they become major players. While they are well-equipped to scale, they are newer entrants to the real estate brokerage business and do not have the institutional experience and real estate savvy many traditional brokerages have refined over decades.

Nevertheless, traditional brokerages must prepare for the emergence of MDBs by elevating their services and more clearly justifying their comparatively high fees. This means recruiting exceptional, entrepreneurial agents who have extensive experience and provide clients with standout service and knowledge. Brokerages should also refine their branding and messaging to clarify just how and why they are worth more than these low-fee firms to justify traditional commission splits, implicitly and explicitly. This can be done, in part, by focusing on creating a local, meaningful brand with marketing that resonates with target prospects.

Create Winning Strategies

T3 Broker Solutions

- Market Research
- Strategic Thinking
- Expansion Strategies
- Mergers & Acquistions
- Tech Solutions
- Business Options
- Future Planning
- Leadership Development

 t360.com

02

Enter the Direct Buyer

Gradual Shift or Far-Reaching Revolution?

Despite revolutionary advances in nearly all facets of real estate, transactions remain notoriously slow, uncertain and tedious — consumer pain points that a new breed of real estate company is looking to alleviate. These firms merge brokerage and finance into a new type of company we call Direct Buyers. Fueled by millions in investor funding, Direct Buyers, also known as iBuyers, have jumped into the real estate arena and are making a big splash, pioneering a model that could dramatically change the way brokerages operate and consumers buy and sell homes.

Trend 02: Enter the Direct Buyer

> "Digital purchases have never been easier than they are today."

Consumers buy furniture on Amazon with one click, get approved for a car loan online in minutes and wave their smartphone instead of swiping a credit card at the grocery store.

Just as in other areas of commerce, Direct Buyers aim to streamline the disjointed real estate transaction process, offering speed and convenience to sellers for a premium fee. Some also provide convenience to buyers by offering seven-day-a-week, all-day access to many of their listings.

Direct Buyers operate as hybrid brokerage-financial firms, which buy properties from sellers and then fix them up and sell them. In-house, or partner agents, typically represent buyers on both sides of the transaction. They differ from the fix-and-flip firms who offer quick cash often at below-market prices to distressed homeowners in need of quick money that have operated in real estate for decades. Instead, these firms strive to make market-rate, or near market-rate offers to more traditional homesellers.

By melding aspects of the home mortgage and lending process with those of a traditional real estate brokerage, Direct Buyers can bypass the long timeliness and hassles many homeowners face when selling their home. Instead, in this new model, sellers indicate their interest, receive an offer and select a move-out date, which can be as soon as a few days from signing a contract. That is convenience compatible with the e-commerce age and the emerging generations used to that type of service. These firms are creating new client expectations and pioneering a new future for the real estate brokerage model.

> "Despite revolutionary advances in nearly all facets of real estate, transactions remain notoriously slow, uncertain and tedious."

Opendoor (opendoor.com), OfferPad (offerpad.com) and Redfin (redfin.com), through its Redfin Now (redfin.com/now) platform, use this business model. Others include Austin, Texas-based Amne (amne.co) and Atlanta-based Knock (knock.com), but they are not covered in this report, which focuses on the larger players and those with larger consumer brands. Zillow Group entered the Direct Buyer arena in 2017 with the test launch of Zillow Instant Offers (zillow.com/instant-offers), which leverages the same basic Direct Buyer concept, but instead of Zillow Group buying homes itself, it connects homesellers with a group of hand-selected investors who often send offers to sellers within two days.

Direct Buyers have initially opened operations in markets with homogenous housing stock such as Phoenix, Atlanta, Las Vegas and Dallas, which helps their pricing engines more accurately price homes and better evaluate housing market trajectories. These firms now operate in at least 10 markets: Phoenix; Dallas; Las Vegas; Atlanta; Orlando, Florida; Tampa, Florida; Raleigh, North Carolina; Charlotte, North Carolina; Salt Lake City; and Los Angeles.

This is a fast-moving phenomenon. The Direct Buyers profiled in this chapter are pioneering a new way for brokerages, agents and consumers to consummate a real estate transaction. The information in this chapter is accurate through November 2017 when this report went to publication. Stay tuned for in-depth updates from T3 Sixty on Direct Buyers in future publications.

How Direct Buyers Work

While the services provided by the Direct Buyers profiled in this chapter vary slightly, they share many features in common. Below is a generalized outline of how they work. This overview does not include Zillow Instant Offers, because the service does not operate as a Direct Buyer itself, but connects sellers to investors.

To make their models work, Direct Buyers focus on specific types of homes. Each specifies the types of homes they will purchase and those they will not. For example, below are the types of homes Redfin Now notes on its site that it will consider purchasing:

- Single-family homes.
- Townhomes or condos pending HOA review.
- Homes built after 1960.
- Total lot size under half an acre.
- Redfin Now estimated value between $150,000 and $550,000.
- Owner-occupied or vacant.
- Clear title.
- Homes in good condition.

The quick generation of an offer is one way that Direct Buyers streamline the transaction process. Direct Buyers use a combination of algorithms and humans to price a home and determine whether it is a good investment. These algorithms consider various factors, including:

- Estimated cost of required repairs.
- Appraisal, inspection and closing costs.
- Staging costs.
- Property tax information.
- Past sales.
- Comparable sales in the home's neighborhood.
- Month-over-month cost of holding the inventory.
- Estimated required time to get the home on the market and sold.
- Any included home warranties or guarantees.
- The estimated final sale price.
- The growth rate in home sales price in the market and neighborhood.

"Direct Buyers aim to streamline the fragmented real estate transaction process."

Because they do not finance their purchases through a mortgage, Direct Buyers bypass the long timelines associated with securing and coordinating lender funds when making a purchase. This is how they can close on homes within days after a seller signs a contract. In addition, Direct Buyers evaluate each home they consider buying and offer to perform repairs for sellers and collect payment for the estimates at closing. This removes any delay associated with sellers prepping a home for sale.

Direct Buyers can also control other parts of the transaction, from selecting the title company to arranging the inspection or providing in-house title and mortgage services. Both Opendoor and Redfin have mortgage and title wings. When Direct Buyers resell homes, they often list them on the MLS to capture attention from the widest possible pool of buyers. Many of their listings include technology that facilitates giving buyers self-serve access to home tours.

Leading Direct Buyers

Currently four major Direct Buyers operate in the U.S. including Zillow Group, which currently serves more as a Direct Buyer middleman than as a Direct Buyer itself. These firms stand out among others in the field based on their significant consumer reach, significant funding, or both. They are: Opendoor, OfferPad, Zillow Group and Redfin.

Direct Buyer Comparison

Company, year founded	Active Markets	Fees	Total funding[1]	Model	Consumer Pitch
Opendoor, 2014	Phoenix, Dallas-Fort Worth; Las Vegas; Atlanta; Orlando, Florida; and Raleigh, North Carolina.	Sellers pay a fee that ranges from 6% to 12% of the sales price. They pay for closing costs and repairs.	$720 million, including debt financing	A licensed brokerage, Opendoor buys homes directly from sellers for a service fee, and then fixes up and sells them. It offers buyers all-day open houses, a one-year home warranty, and the option to return their home within 30 days.	"Get an offer on your home with the press of a button."
OfferPad, 2015	Phoenix; Los Angeles; Atlanta; Salt Lake City; Las Vegas; Tampa, Florida; Orlando, Florida; and Charlotte, North Carolina.	Sellers pay a 6% agency fee and a service fee that ranges from 1% to 7% of the sale price, depending on the home's condition and other factors. Sellers pay for repairs and closing costs.	$260 million, including debt financing	A licensed brokerage, OfferPad buys homes directly from sellers, prepares them for resale and then lists and sells them on the open market.	"We're ready to buy your home: Click. Sold. Move."
Redfin Now[2], 2016	Undisclosed.	Sellers pay a fee of from 7% to 9% of the sales price. They pay closing costs and repairs.	Parent company Redfin funds the test.	A subsidiary of Redfin, Redfin Now buys homes directly from sellers, and then fixes them up and sells them. Sellers request offers online; after scheduling a home visit, Redfin Now makes an offer.	"Sell your home, hassle-free."
Zillow Instant Offers[2], 2017	Las Vegas, Phoenix and Orlando, Florida.	No participation fees currently charged by Zillow	Parent company Zillow Group funds the test.	Zillow Instant Offers connects homesellers with investors willing to make all-cash offers on their homes and real estate agents who provide professional valuations.	"Get offers with just a few clicks."

Source: Zillow Group, Redfin, OfferPad, Opendoor
[1] Through November 2017.
[2] Companies characterize their programs as a test.

Opendoor

Silicon Valley heavyweight Keith Rabois, former chief operating officer of financial services startup Square and a partner at vaunted venture capital firm Khosla Ventures (khoslaventures.com), founded Opendoor in 2014 with former Trulia exec Eric Wu and a few other experienced technologists. Rabois serves as Opendoor's executive chairman and Wu as CEO. The San

Francisco-based firm has pulled in over $320 million in equity funding since launch and $720 million if debt financing is included.

The company's deep Silicon Valley roots have helped it secure top-notch investor and lender backing; investors include Wells Fargo (wellsfargo.com), Deutsche Bank (db.com/usa), Norwest Ventures (nvp.com), GGV Capital (ggvc.com) and Khosla Ventures. The firm is valued at over $1 billion. For more on the recent role outside investors have played in revolutionizing the industry, see Trend No. 1, "Follow the Money."

Opendoor is a licensed brokerage and uses salaried in-house agents on both sides of the transactions it does. The firm does not disclose detailed operating data, but an independent analysis indicated that the company captured about made about $8,000 in profit in each home sale in Phoenix through December 2016 after accounting for repairs, commissions and other expenses.

Active Markets
Opendoor started buying homes in Phoenix in late 2014 and as of November 2017 operates in six markets: Phoenix; Dallas-Fort Worth, Texas; Las Vegas; Atlanta; Raleigh, North Carolina; and Orlando, Florida. It has announced plans to expand to 30 markets by the end of 2018.

> "The firm delivers an offer often within 24 hours; the offer is good for five days."

How it Works
Opendoor buys homes directly from sellers who request an offer from its website after answering a few questions about their home. The firm delivers an offer often within 24 hours; the offer is good for five days. When sellers accept an offer, they schedule a time for an Opendoor representative to inspect the home, which can be as soon as the same day sellers accept an offer.

After the firm determines needed repairs, it adds an estimate for repairs when it draws up a contract for sellers to review. Sellers can choose to credit the firm that amount at closing or they can perform the repairs themselves before moving out. At this point in the process, sellers can still walk away from the transaction. From the day sellers sign the contract, they can choose to move out any time from three to 60 days. Opendoor also offers sellers the ability to trade in their home for one in Opendoor's inventory.

The firm offers buyers the following services:

- All-day open houses, 9 a.m. – 6 p.m., seven days a week.

- A one-year home warranty from OneGuard Home Warranties (oneguardhomewarranty.com) that covers an array of potential home issues and includes a $69 service call fee.

- A 30-day satisfaction guarantee that allows buyers to sell back homes they purchase from the firm if they are not satisfied. Opendoor will return the full purchase price "less any costs associated with repairing any damages" that might have occurred between closing and the request to sell back the home. If the market dips beyond a threshold Opendoor specifies, it may refuse a buy-back request.

Opendoor's transaction service charge starts at 6 percent of the purchase price and increases depending on the individual home and transaction; the firm says its service fee averaged 6.7 percent in September 2017.

How Agents Fit In

Opendoor is licensed as a brokerage and uses in-house listing agents to sell the homes in its inventory. It also uses in-house agents at times to buy homes.

Opendoor currently partners with outside real estate agents in three ways:

- Agents who refer sellers to Opendoor receive a 1 percent referral fee.

- Listing agents representing sellers who want to use Opendoor can work with the company directly. The company says it will honor all pre-existing listing agreements when a deal closes, which likely takes the form of sellers paying their agent on top of any Opendoor fees.

- Opendoor makes its listed properties available to agents representing buyers and offers them a full market-rate commission on closing.

OfferPad

Real estate agent Brian Bair and Jerry Coleman, co-founder of Blackstone's single-family rental investment vertical Invitation Homes (invitationhomes.com), founded OfferPad in 2015 and run the firm as co-CEOs. Like Opendoor, OfferPad purchases homes directly from sellers with a streamlined online offer system and then makes any necessary repairs and sells the homes itself. It has raised $260 million in equity and debt funding since launch.

Like Opendoor, OfferPad is a licensed brokerage and uses in-house agents on both its list- and buy-side transactions.

Markets

OfferPad operates in eight markets and has expressed plans to expand to Houston and Nashville, Tennessee. Its current markets include: Phoenix; Los Angeles; Tampa, Florida; Orlando, Florida; Atlanta; Las Vegas; Charlotte, North Carolina; and Salt Lake City. In early December 2017, it had 213 listings in Phoenix; 110 listings in Tampa, Florida; and 44 listings in Orlando, Florida.

How it Works

Like Opendoor, sellers request an offer from OfferPad by typing in their address on its website. The firm emails sellers an offer within one business day; the offer is good for 48 hours. If sellers have a listing agent, the firm sends the offer to their agent. When sellers accept the offer, OfferPad sends a contract for them to digitally sign; they then choose a close date from five to 90 days. Next, the firm opens escrow with a title company and deposits earnest money and coordinates with sellers on scheduling a home inspection.

In addition to a quick offer and the ability to set their own move-out date, the company offers free moving services to sellers who pack their own belongings and move within 50 miles.

OfferPad charges sellers a traditional agency fee of 6 percent of the home's sale price, comparable to the amount agents pay to agents in a traditional sale. On top of this, it charges a service fee that ranges from 1 to 7 percent of the home's sale price; a home's condition and other factors determine the service fee level.

Buyers can use OfferPad technology to tour many of the firm's listings themselves. During the tour, they can view home details and make an online offer. In addition, homebuyers can request buyer-agent services on-demand; in these cases, OfferPad connects them with a local agent who then serves them.

How Agents Fit In

The company pays agents a 1 percent referral fee for referring unrepresented sellers who end up closing with the company. Buyer's agents who participate in its agent-on-demand service receive a 1 percent commission when they help a buyer purchase an OfferPad home. It also offers agents the ability to partner with the firm, which includes the ability to receive listing referrals from the firm on homes that do not meet its purchase guidelines.

Zillow Instant Offers

In May 2017, Zillow Group began testing a Direct Buyer service, Instant Offers, in two markets. With Instant Offers, Zillow does not currently purchase homes directly from sellers, but that will most likely change in 2018.

Currently Zillow enables sellers to receive a comparative market analysis (CMA) from a real estate agent in addition to offers from investors. Zillow then connects the seller with the agent-represented investor or real estate agent, depending on the seller's preferences. If the seller opts for an investor offer, Zillow recommends that the seller use agent representation.

Active Markets

As of November 2017, Zillow Instant Offers was available in three test markets. In Las Vegas and Orlando, Florida, Zillow sends Instant Offer seller leads to agent advertisers from multiple brokerages. In August 2017, the firm expanded its test to Phoenix, where the firm sends seller leads exclusively to two brokerages, who then distribute to their agents as they see fit.

How it Works

Sellers request an offer from the Zillow Instant Offers website by sharing basic information about their home and uploading photos. Investors send sellers cash offers through the Instant Offers platform — sometimes more than one investor from among Zillow's stable of participating investors in the seller's area send an offer within 48 hours. Sellers also receive an

Direct Buyer Vs. Traditional Sale

Opendoor and OfferPad (and other Direct Buyers) appeal to consumers on speed-to-close, certainty and convenience. The companies also claim that sellers can net more dollars through their service than a traditional sale if repairs and holding costs are taken into consideration.

	Direct Buyer[1]	**Traditional Sale**
Days to close	Choose from 5 to 60 days[2]	2–3 months
Days to prep and stage home	0 days	1–2 weeks
Showings	0 showings	1–10 showings
Fee	6%–12%[3]	5%–6%[3]

Source: Opendoor, OfferPad, T3 Sixty
[1] Direct Buyers consider only certain types of homes and present a nonnegotiable offer.
[2] Varies by Direct Buyer.
[3] Typical range.

agent-produced home valuation (if an unrepresented seller) at the same time. Sellers then choose whether to accept an offer from one of the investors, choose the agent who provided the CMA or another agent, or decline to move forward.

If sellers choose one of the investor offers, a licensed inspector comes out and assesses the home and identifies needed repairs, which will affect the final purchase price the investor pays. Once a contract is signed, a deal can close in as little as seven days.

As of November 2017, Zillow Group does not charge investors or homebuyers to participate in the program.

One third of the leads generated by the Zillow Instant Offers program wind up selling a home, according to Zillow Group. Early program results reveal that sellers are overwhelmingly choosing to list with an agent, which has made it a valuable seller leads source for its participating agent and brokerage advertisers in the test markets.

How Agents Fit In
Zillow Instant Offers investors are required to use a licensed real estate agent and sellers are encouraged to use an agent to represent them. Participating brokers and agents must be Zillow Group advertisers.

Redfin Now

Redfin made headlines in 2017 with a July initial public offering that landed the firm $138 million in funding and exposed its tech-focused brokerage model to the industry. Launched in 2006, the Seattle-based brokerage operates a new-era discount brokerage model in major markets in all 50 states. Read more about these types of brokerages in Trend No. 3, "The Rise of the Modern Discount Brokerage."

As part of the disclosures it made in conjunction with its IPO, Redfin revealed that it has quietly been piloting a Direct Buyer operation, Redfin Now, that, like Opendoor and OfferPad, purchases homes directly from sellers. As of June 30, 2017, the firm had spent $1.8 million on Redfin Now; the firm is still testing the service.

Active Markets
Redfin Now is currently active in several undisclosed markets. Based on "success stories" presented on the Redfin Now website, two of those markets were Murrieta and Winchester, California, which are located about 80 miles east of Los Angeles.

Direct Buyer Consumer Profile

Factors other than sales price have always appealed to a segment of sellers. These sellers are willing to walk away with less money from their home sale if they can control the timeline and are not inconvenienced by the process. Direct Buyers target these sellers.

Factors important to homesellers beyond sale price, can include:

- Divorce, death or another life change that necessitates a quicker sale.

- Financial circumstances that have an immediacy that cannot be delayed for weeks or months.

- A desire to avoid repairs, photography, staging, showing or other aspects of the sales process that many sellers find stressful and inconvenient.

- A need to tightly control the transaction closing or moving timeline.

- The convenience of securing a sales price and timeline without negotiating with a buyer or hiring an agent.

- A desire to avoid the cleaning, repair, showing, and negotiation processes of a traditional sale.

Buyers may be attracted to the easy ability to tour Direct Buyer homes on their schedule. Some also may appreciate features such as Opendoor's 30-day, money-back guarantee, but most have enough challenges finding a home at the right price and will likely not restrict themselves to Direct Buyer listings. But if these models continue to gain traction, they could develop financing products and other transaction-streamlining services that could increase their buyer appeal.

How it Works

Redfin Now sellers request an offer using the Redfin Now website. After completing a home visit, the company makes an offer within 48 hours and includes a home repair estimate. If the sellers accept the offer, they can choose a closing date from between seven and 60 days. After purchase, Redfin Now makes repairs and upgrades as it sees fit before relisting the home.

Redfin Now charges sellers between 7 and 9 percent of the home's sale price for its service. The firm breaks this fee into two categories: a fixed convenience fee of 6 percent and a market-risk fee that ranges from 1 to 3 percent based on how long the firm expects it will take to sell the home and other factors.

As Redfin explains in its S-1 registration statement, "Customers who sell through Redfin Now will typically get less money for their home than they would listing their home with a real estate agent, but get that money faster with less risk and fuss."

The firm has not disclosed any services for buyers.

How Agents Fit in

Listing agents can request a Redfin Now offer on their clients' behalf. If represented sellers wants to sell their home to Redfin Now, they will have to pay their agent themselves out of the proceeds from their home sale.

As Redfin Now is a wholly-owned subsidiary of Redfin, a full-fledged brokerage with salaried agents across the country, it is likely that Redfin Now leverages or will leverage Redfin agents to help close transactions and to relist properties under the Redfin brand.

Direct Buyer Outlook

Traction

Both Opendoor and OfferPad have seen market share grow in their respective cities. Double-digit growth is impressive, but growth is always big when companies start out. In the next year, it will become clearer whether these firms are poised for significant market penetration or nearing market saturation.

Early signs suggest that these models are just getting started. In October, Opendoor announced that it was buying homes at a clip of $100 million per month. The same month, Opendoor's CEO Eric Wu told Forbes that the firm had over a 3 percent market share in Phoenix and Dallas markets, having increased from 2 percent share the year before. These cities are the first the Direct Buyer began operating in and its biggest markets. (It launched in Phoenix in 2014 and Dallas-Fort Worth in 2015).

Risks

Like all brokerages, Direct Buyers are sensitive to significant market shifts. Unlike other businesses, however, these companies own their inventory and thus face great risk if market changes make it more difficult to sell homes or cause prices to drop significantly. Zillow Group is more insulated from this risk because it currently serves as a middleman between homesellers and investors; it does not own any real estate. For the other Direct Buyer participants, the risks loom much larger.

A Direct Buyer's ability to generate a profit in a strong housing market is contingent on the accuracy of its pricing engine. There also may not be many sellers in a particular market interested in sacrificing their home's exposure to a wide array of buyers for the convenience of an expedited sale. Based on specific market dynamics, some areas will naturally be more attractive to Direct Buyers than others.

> "These companies own their inventory and thus face great risk if market changes make it more difficult to sell homes or cause prices to drop significantly."

Sellers face a risk selling to a Direct Buyer because they miss the opportunity to expose their homes to a wide segment of buyers the MLS and other platforms provide. They end up not only paying a service fee to Direct Buyers but also potentially forego the opportunity to get a higher price on the open market.

Opportunities

A segment of sellers in many markets will prioritize convenience, speed and security above receiving the highest possible sales price on their home. If a Direct Buyer can tap into this segment and become a preferred choice for these sellers, it can capture transaction fees and a profit from reselling these homes after repairs and updates. Zillow Group's Instant Offers service has an opportunity to establish itself as a new marketplace that connects sellers with buyers, and opens up a potential new revenue stream for the media giant. Silicon Valley has clearly demonstrated its excitement about the potential

"Traditional real estate players should expect to share market space with the Direct Buyer platform."

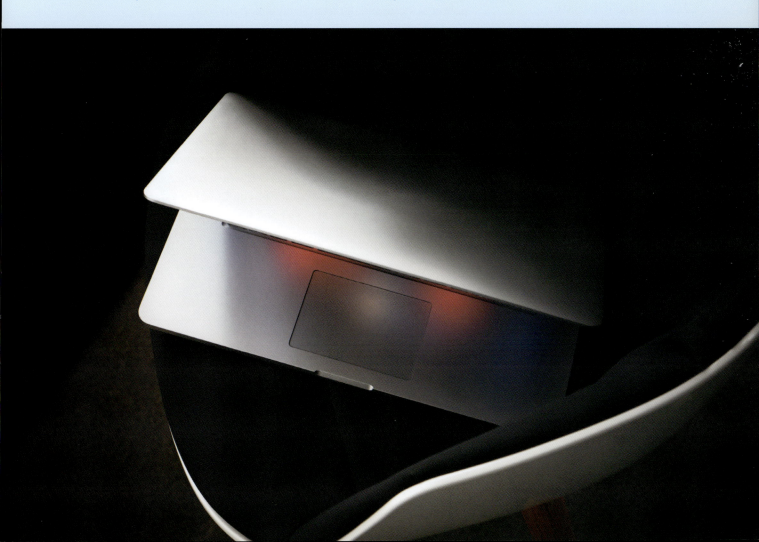

for Direct Buyer business models to generate large returns. Few other residential real estate technologies have gained the same attention and funding from investors. The fact that established real estate companies are beginning to test the Direct Buyer model appears to validate this trend.

As digital natives come of age, begin forming households and families and start to become homeowners, Direct Buyer platforms may become appealing to a larger segment of real estate consumers. Time will tell how upcoming generations will view the value of the convenience and certainty these models provide relative to their additional cost.

"Silicon Valley has clearly demonstrated its excitement about the potential for Direct Buyer business models to generate large returns."

Takeaway

The amount of capital infused into the new Direct Buyer business model and the buzz around its hot startups Opendoor and OfferPad have caught the industry's attention, including industry players Zillow Group and Redfin who have jumped into Direct Buyer fray. While grabbing headlines and investor cash, this business model's staying power and impact will depend on whether a significant percentage of sellers will opt for convenience and speed over potential increased net returns on their home sale.

Brokerages or real estate teams who focus on quick, expedient transaction experiences may find themselves competing more for listing clients with Direct Buyers than brokerages that emphasize their marketing programs or list-to-sale ratios.

Understanding the Direct Buyer movement, the fees they charge and how they work will help brokers and agents discuss options with sellers, how best to effectively position their services and when, perhaps, to work with a Direct Buyer. They can also strategically leverage Direct Buyers as all-cash buyers on homes they find difficult to sell or if their sellers need to make a quick sale.

T3 Fellows

Mentoring brokerages and teams to transform their firms into best-in-class businesses.

Next enrollment: Spring 2018.

t3fellows.com
t360.com

01

Follow the Money

Investors Fueling a Real Estate Tech Revolution

Real estate is a diverse industry that drives a big portion of America's economic engine, accounting for nearly a fifth of the U.S.'s annual gross domestic product. It represents a huge opportunity for the professional investors, primarily venture capital firms, who have turned their eyes toward real estate in recent years. Attracted by the opportunity to capitalize on the industry's slow tech adoption, they are placing big bets in the hopes of large returns and rapidly reshaping the industry in the process.

Professional Investors Turn Eyes Toward Real Estate

Editor's note: Unless otherwise noted, 2017 data complete through Dec. 7

Until a few years ago investors from outside the industry have not poured significant money into real estate technology as they have in other industries. But that is changing – outside money is catalyzing a rapid tech-powered revolution in the industry. Investment in real estate tech has increased every year over the last five years, jumping more than threefold from $383 million in 2013 to $2 billion in 2017. Investor real estate tech funding is growing and shows no signs of slowing down.

This investment is spurring increased innovation and transforming the real estate industry with digital tools that automate lead generation and followup, spur new brokerage business models and provide new ways for consumers to shop for homes with 3D modeling and augmented reality. This chapter outlines the types of technology receiving funding, who is investing and some of the companies participating.

Types of Investment

Funding for startups can come from a variety of sources in two distinct types: private sources such as company principals, family and friends, angel investors, venture capital firms, other companies, lenders and banks; and public sources such as a public stock exchange like the New York Stock Exchange and the Nasdaq Stock Market.

Regardless of whether funding is public or private, it comes in two flavors: debt or equity. In debt funding, a startup takes on debt (just as individuals do with credit cards or mortgages) under specific terms, interest rates and liquidation schedules (the order of who gets paid back first). Equity funding covers instances where investors make a cash contribution to a startup in exchange for a share of the company in the hopes of participating in its future success. Anyone who buys shares in a public company is buying equity, for example; the same is true with venture capital firms. Just as with debt, equity shares have liquidation schedules and sometimes include other features such as oversight rights (the ability to dictate board of director seats, approval of a sale and more).

Investor Interest in Real Estate

Investment in real estate technology has grown steadily over the last five years with a significant recent uptick in investments in later-stage real estate tech companies, which means investors are taking bigger investment swings. Two 2017 funding events illustrate the larger trend: tech-focused brokerage Compass' (compass.com) game-changing December 2017 $450 million Series F round and agent tech platform provider Placester's (placester.com) March 2017 $50 million Series D round.

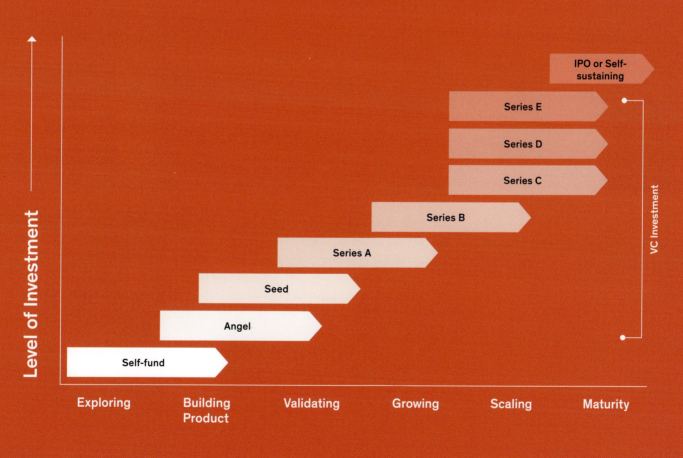

Source: T3 Sixty

A growing interest and participation from blue blood venture capital firms such as Andreesen Horowitz (a16z.com) and Kleiner Perkins Caufield & Byers (kpcb.com) indicates the growing interest of institutional investors in real estate tech. After revamping other industries slow to adapt to technology such as travel, rising home prices and rents in the wake of the Great Recession contribute to real estate's allure for VCs, whose business centers on spotting tech companies poised for huge valuation growth.

In exchange for investments at early stages in these startups, VCs often take a percentage of the company. They are making a bet that the value of that initial stake will balloon to many multiples as the firm matures and its valuation increases. VC firms' increased focus on real estate has created a frothy investment environment in the industry.

Venture Capital Firms

Venture capital firms (VCs) account for real estate's recent uptick in outside investment. They played a big role in the dot-com era of the early 2000s and provide startup or growth funds in the form of equity or debt funding with the hope of making returns that trump market interest rates. VCs garner massive funds from investors who become limited partners; these partners tend to be large corporations, family funds, pension funds, charitable organizations, endowments and insurance companies. They typically invest across multiple industries. VCs typically evaluate opportunities based on the quality and experience of the management team, strategy and business model, product and technology, attractiveness of the market, customer adoption, competition, as well as valuation and fit with VC mission and focus.

Opendoor's (opendoor.com) $210 million round in 2016 is a good example of blue blood VCs betting big on real estate. Eleven investors participated in the hot, growing Direct Buyer's round including blue-chip VCs Khosla Ventures (khoslaventures.com) and New Enterprise Associates (nea.com) and the relatively new real estate-focused fund Fifth Wall (fifthwall.vc). For more on Direct Buyers, see Trend No. 2, "Enter the Direct Buyer."

The industry's tech landscape remains extremely fragmented. Investment is spread over hundreds of technology companies of all stages with a wide variety of functionalities. The absence of dominant players with large market share has created opportunity for new players to break into the market, secure a beachhead and potentially generate large returns for investors.

Where Is The Money Going?

The $2 billion investment in U.S. real estate technology in 2017 exceeds the amount invested in 2016 by 87 percent. The U.S. real estate technology funding landscape includes software tools and platforms used by agents, brokerages, investors, consumers, lenders and mortgage providers, and property owners and managers. This definition does not include sharing technology services, property owners or broad multi-industry services such as Airbnb (airbnb.com), WeWork (wework.com) or DocuSign (docusign.com).

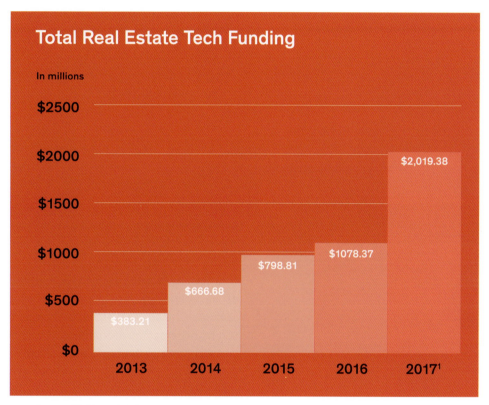

Source: T3 Sixty with Crunchbase data
[1] Through Dec. 7.

Real estate technology investment can be categorized into three primary categories — Residential, Mortgage and Commercial, with funding in the residential category accounting for 79 percent of the $2 billion funding in 2017. Residential tech funding more than tripled between 2016 and 2017.

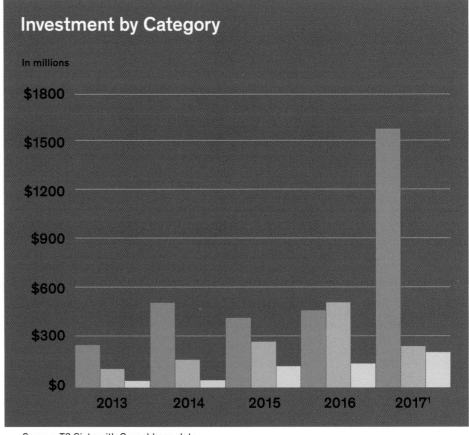

Investment by Category
In millions

- Residential
- Commercial
- Mortgage

Source: T3 Sixty with Crunchbase data
[1] Through Dec. 7.

This chapter focuses on the U.S. market, but note that substantial real estate technology investment is occurring globally, particularly in China. For example, Chinese real estate brokerage Home Link (lianjia.com) and transaction management platform FangDD (fangdd.com), have raised over $1 billion and $313 million through Dec. 7, 2017, respectively.

Residential

Recent funding indicates investors are interested in innovations that improve functionality both within residential real estate's existing business models and those pushing the frontiers. Even disregarding the June 2017 $400 million funding round by digital home design and staging site Houzz (houzz.com) and Compass's December $450 million funding round, 2017 investment in the residential category has trumped full-year investments in each of the four previous years.

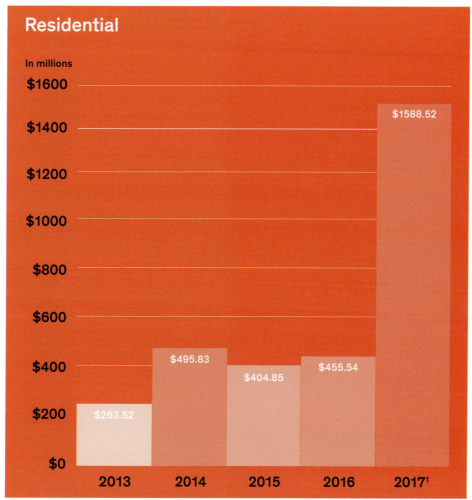

Source: T3 Sixty with Crunchbase data
[1] Through Dec. 7.

Digging into recent investments, three major themes emerge: tech-centric brokerage models, data and predictive analytics and augmented reality and 3D imaging. (For more on tech-centric brokerage models, see Trend No. 3, "Rise of the Modern Discount Brokerage.")

Tech-centric Brokerage Models

Investment in tech-centric brokerage models is a major area of residential real estate funding. Venture investment in companies in this field measures over $1.1 billion from 2016 through Dec. 7, 2017.

"The real estate industry still has immense room for technology innovation."

Tech-focused brokerage Compass' December 2017 $450 million Series F funding, following shortly after a $100 million November Series E round, illustrates the type of investment investors are making in the category. Compass investors include top-grade VC Founders Fund (foundersfund.com) and Goldman Sachs (goldmansachs.com), with the most recent round funded by SoftBank Capital (softbankvc.com). The rounds gave the well-funded, 5-year-old brokerage that bills itself as the architect of the "first modern real estate platform," a post-money valuation of $2.2 billion. Since its 2013 launch, the New York City-based firm has grown to over 2,000 agents, 11 markets across the country and reports annual revenues north of $300 million.

Seattle-based Redfin (redfin.com), which has not raised private money since a 2014 $70.9 million round, raised $138 million in July 2017 when it went public on the Nasdaq stock exchange. In December 2017, the company's market cap had climbed to $2 billion, representing a 65 percent jump in share price in five months as a public company.

By using technology to streamline and reduce costs of the traditional real estate process, tech companies are launching alternative brokerage models with the help of investors. Opendoor, a pioneer of a new type of brokerage that buys homes directly from sellers and then sells them on the open market, is perhaps the most well-known and well-funded. (Read more about these models in Trend No. 2, "Enter the Direct Buyer.") It raised $210 million in a Series D round in late 2016 giving it a post-money valuation of $1.1 billion. Opendoor investors include VCs Khosla Ventures and Fifth Wall.

OfferPad (offerpad.com), another Direct Buyer, raised $260 million in debt and equity financing in 2017, indicating that alternative broker model technology companies are a hot investor commodity. A third big player in the space, Knock (knock.co), raised $32.5 million in 2017 in a Series A raise, which included participation from first-class VC Redpoint Ventures (redpoint.com).

Data and Predictive Analytics
A second theme in the residential category covers startups that offer data and predictive analytics tools. HouseCanary (housecanary.com) raised two rounds in 2017 for a total of $64 million. Investors include Google's Eric Schmidt and PSP Growth (investpsp.com/en), a division of the investment firm founded by former U.S. Secretary of Commerce Penny Pritzker. Real estate investors, firms and mortgage lenders use HouseCanary's data and predictive analytics to estimate and evaluate property values for themselves and their clients.

Other companies receiving funding provide predictive analytics services that focus on identifying or qualifying leads. For example, SmartZip (smartzip.com), which launched in 2008 and has raised $30.6 million

> "Investors are taking bigger investment swings in real estate."

has tools that help agents pinpoint which homeowners in their farms are most likely to sell soon. More recent entrants have raised early-stage funding or undisclosed amounts including First (first.io) and Remine (remine.com). First and Remine offer predictive analytics products that help their customers identify contacts in their databases who are most likely to transact, with a goal of making real estate agent marketing dollars more efficient. (To read more about these and related tech firms, see Trend No. 8, "Smart CRMs Go Mainstream.")

SmartZip, First and Remine each have notable agent, broker and MLS customers, indicating the market's desire for this type of product. No firm has emerged as a dominant market share winner yet.

Augmented Reality and 3D Imaging

Matterport (matterport.com) represents the third major investment theme in the residential category — augmented reality and 3D. Many real estate agents and brokers will recognize the Matterport brand as it has become a popular tool to create and display immersive 3D virtual tours of homes for sale, particularly those in higher price ranges. Over 200,000 real estate listings in 2017 had a Matterport tour 2017, according to the startup. Matterport has raised a total of $66 million, including a $35 million Series C round in 2015 and two subsequent rounds that included a strategic investment from News Corp., owner of realtor.com operator Move Inc. and global luxury home site Mansion Global.

Another virtual real estate model provider, Rooomy (rooomy.com) has also attracted investors. The startup, which provides 3D modeling and augmented reality-powered virtual staging service to real estate agents, home furnishing companies and interior designers, has raised $13 million through November 2017 since its 2010 launch.

Real estate tech giant Zillow Group made its first outside investment in July 2017 when it led a $10 million Series A round for Hutch Interiors (hutch.com), an app that uses augmented reality to facilitate virtual staging and design. Until this investment, Zillow Groups investments took the form of acquisitions.

Home décor and remodeling firm Houzz raised a $400 million round in June 2017, making it the far-and-away leader of this area of real estate funding. Houzz notes that it will use the funding to invest in geographic expansion and technology. For example, Houzz introduced the "View in My Room 3D" tool in 2017 that allows consumers to design and experience a room's layout by adding multiple 3D products to a virtual space. Houzz makes money from consumers who purchase furniture and décor products, but as it continues to develop technology in this space, watch for it to jump into products for professionals as well. Its massive funding round and sky-high valuation indicates how lucrative investors believe the home décor and improvement vertical can be.

Mortgage

Mortgage is a significant vertical in the U.S. The Mortgage Bankers Association expects mortgage originations alone to reach $1.63 trillion in 2017. The category has attracted significant attention and investment from top venture capital funds. Investment in mortgage technology ramped up significantly in 2015, remained high in 2016 and took another step up in 2017.

Mortgage investment in 2017 of $198 million through Dec. 7 was $76 million higher than all of 2016. In 2016 and 2017, the bulk of investment dollars went to two types of mortgage technology: mortgage processing and workflow technology, and digital lenders. The focused investment, especially in later-stage companies, may spur a race for customer adoption to establish a clear leader in the space.

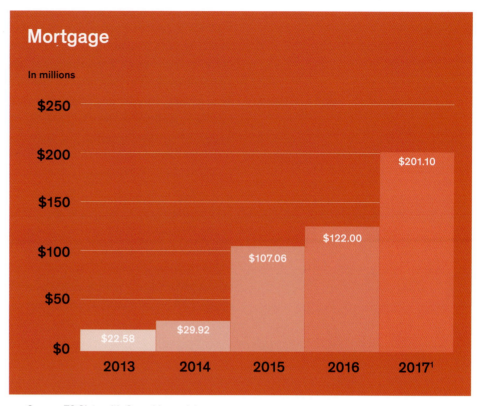

Source: T3 Sixty with Crunchbase data
[1] Through Dec. 7.

Mortgage Processing and Workflow Technology

Mortgage processing and workflow technology streamlines the mortgage process from application to close and facilitates communication among lenders, mortgage agents, real estate agents and consumers. These technologies address two key pain points in the mortgage process: visibility and long timelines.

With raises of $100 million and $40 million in 2017 and 2016, respectively, Blend Labs (blend.com) is the most well-funded startup in this category. A mortgage technology that streamlines mortgage workflows from application to closing and facilitates communication among all parties of the mortgage process, Blend has attracted investment from a handful of blue-chip VCs including Andreessen Horowitz, Greylock Partners (greylock.com) and Lightspeed Venture Partners (lsvp.com). It recently announced partnerships with both Wells Fargo (wellsfargo.com) and U.S. Bank (usbank.com). Cloudvirga's (cloudvirga.com) processing and workflow technology, which was first developed at lender Skyline Home Loans and spun off in 2016, has raised $22.5 million in two rounds through November 2017.

Other startups aiming to streamline mortgage workflow include Maxwell (himaxwell.com), MortgageHippo (mortgagehippo.com) and Approved (getapproved.io) each raising $1 to 5 million in seed funding in 2016 and 2017 through Dec. 7.

Digital Lenders

Digital lenders, like mortgage processing and workflow technology providers, offer technology that streamlines the mortgage process and increases its transparency but go a step further by funding the loans themselves, at least initially. This extra funding step allows digital lenders to earn revenue from the loans themselves and potentially take a larger piece of the mortgage pie than they would as just technology providers alone.

LendingHome (lendinghome.com), a prominent player in this space, raised $57 million in October 2017, bringing its total funding to $166 million with participation from blue-chip VC First Round Capital (firstround.com). Digital lender Better Mortgage (better.com) raised $45 million in 2016 and 2017 from leading investors Goldman Sachs, IA Ventures (iaventures.com) and Kleiner Perkins Caufield & Byers. Clara Lending (clara.com), another digital lender, raised $24.3 million in 2016, which included participation from top-grade VC Redpoint Ventures (redpoint.com).

"Investor real estate tech funding is growing and shows no signs of slowing down."

Crowdfunding Platforms Dominate Commercial Real Estate Funding

Commercial category funding was down in 2017 through Dec. 7 after double- and triple-digit growth in 2015 and 2016, respectively. Three service categories have received the majority of funding over the last three years: investor crowdfunding platforms, property and building management and leasing-management software. For more insight on the commercial category, please see Trend No. 9, "The Complex World of Commercial Real Estate."

Investor crowdfunding platforms have been a popular investor focus since 2015; companies in this category have received over $100 million each of the last three years. In 2017, crowdfunding was the only significant commercial real estate category. Some crowdfunding platforms such as RealtyShares make residential real estate investment available to nontraditional investors.
Crowdfunding platforms enable investors to finance real estate of all types at a variety of price points, including extremely low ones; some platforms open up the market to noninstitutional investors. For example, Cadre (cadre.com), which has raised $133 million over the last three years including $65 million in 2017, connects investors who have a minimum of $100,000 to invest to over $15 million of commercial real estate investment opportunities. Jared Kushner, President Trump's son-in-law, and his brother Joshua co-founded the company and are reportedly only advisors today. Notable investors include Andreessen Horowitz (a16z.com), Goldman Sachs, Khosla Ventures, General Catalyst (generalcatalyst.com) and Founders Fund.

Where Is The Money Coming From?

As category-agnostic venture funds and incubators begin to pour money into real estate in recognition of technology's potential to revolutionize both transactions and business, more real estate-focused funds and accelerators are also cropping up. In some cases, real estate companies themselves are making investments in startups beyond the traditional form of acquisitions.

Non-Real Estate VCs and Incubators

Most venture firms invest in multiple categories. Until recently, top VCs have not particularly focused on investing in the real estate vertical. But now, VCs widely recognized as the cream of the crop, based on past successes and overall reputation, are getting involved in the real estate space in a big way. The investment analysis firm CB Insights has delineated 24 top VCs based on their investment track record into a group it calls Smart Money VCs. Many firms on this list have begun focusing on real estate including: Andreessen

Other crowdfunding platforms also bring real estate investing to accredited investors but expand availability beyond high-net-worth investors. These companies have minimum investments that range between $1,000 to $5,000.

They are:

- **RealtyShares** (realtyshares.com) is a crowdfunding platform for both commercial and residential real estate. RealtyShares has raised a total of $105.6 million, including a $40 million round of debt and equity in 2017. (Series C). Investors include General Catalyst and Union Square Ventures (usv.com).

- **Roofstock** (roofstock.com) provides a platform for investing leased single-family rental homes. It has raised $68.3 million, including a $35 million in 2017. Khosla Ventures and Lightspeed Venture Partners (lsvp.com) are among Roofstock's largest investors.

- **Realty Mogul** (realtymogul.com) has $46.6 million, with its most recent formal round in 2015 at $35 million.

- **Patch of Land** (patchofland.com) is for borrowers seeking funding for rehabbing properties. The firm has raised $24.9 million with its most recent raise in 2015 at $23.6 million.

- **PeerStreet** (peerstreet.com), an online marketplace where investors invest in private real estate loans, has raised $21.1 million since launching in 2013. Andreessen Horowitz led its $15 million Series A round in 2016.

> "VC firms' increased focus on real estate has created a frothy investment environment in the industry."

Horowitz, New Enterprise Associates, Kleiner Perkins Caufield & Byers, Greylock Partners and Founders Fund.

All but six Smart Money VCs have invested in real estate tech startups since 2013; the 18 who have are listed below.

Smart Money VC Firm	Real Estate-Specfic Investments	Notable Investments Outside Real Estate
Andreessen Horowitz	Zumper, Blend, Cadre, PeerStreet, Point, Pro.com	Airbnb, Box, Facebook, Groupon, Slack, Twitter
New Enterprise Associates	Opendoor, Placester, 42 Floors, Houzz, ISGN Enterprises	Groupon, Box, Care.com
First Round Capital	Clara Lending	Birchbox, Mint, Warby Parker
Accel Partners	Amitree, Floored	Facebook, Etsy, Spotify
True Ventures	Opendoor	Fitbit, Ring
Khosla Ventures	Opendoor, Roofstock, Cadre, Castle	Square, Yammer
General Catalyst Partners	Cadre, Cozy, RealtyShares	Airbnb, Kayak, ClassPass
Kleiner Perkins Caufield & Byers	Zumper, Better Mortgage, Houzz, Riley, Zaarly	Airbnb, Nest, Spotify, Twitter, Uber, Waze
Greylock Partners	Redfin, Zumper, Matterport, Blend, LiquidSpace	Airbnb, Facebook, LinkedIn, GoFundMe, Nextdoor
Floodgate	LiquidSpace	TaskRabbit
Foundry Group	PivotDesk	Fitbit, Zynga
Bessemer Venture Partners	42 Floors, Hightower, VTS	Blue Apron, LinkedIn, Pinterest, Yelp
Lightspeed Venture Partners	Blend, Roofstock, Zaarly	Nest, Stitch Fix, TaskRabbit
Founders Fund	Compass, Estately, Hutch, Porch, Blend	Facebook, Lyft, Spotify
Social Capital	Approved, Cozy, Rescour, Riley	Box, Slack, Survey Monkey
Redpoint Ventures	Clara Lending, Knock, Pro.com	HomeAway, Nextdoor
Union Square Ventures	Flip, RealtyShares	Etsy, Zynga
Emergence Capital Partners	Blend	Box, Yammer

Source: T3 Sixty with Crunchbase data.

> "Real estate brokerages and franchisors and large real estate technology companies are also now investing in or partnering with real estate-focused venture funds."

Real estate is also gaining popularity among national incubators such as 500 Startups (500.co). Thirteen companies in the T3 Sixty U.S. real estate technology landscape analysis have participated in a 500 Startup Seed or Series A program or received investment from the 500 Startups venture fund, including residential-focused firms HomeLight (homelight.com) and Contactually (contactually.com), and commercial technology companies VTS and RealtyShares.

Real Estate Industry Strategic Initiatives

Companies outside real estate are not the only ones taking notice and investing. Real estate brokerages and franchisors and large real estate technology companies are also now investing in or partnering with real estate-focused venture funds and accelerators and investing directly in early- to mid-stage technology companies.

For example, Move Inc. might have looked to acquire a firm such as virtual tour tech firm Matterport in years past; instead, it became an investor in 2016 when its parent company News Corp. made a strategic investment in the firm. The same is true for Zillow Group's 2017 equity investment in augmented reality technology company Hutch Interiors. The increased availability of investment dollars gives more leverage to startups, allowing them to encourage investments rather than acquisitions from larger, strategic partners.

Strategic venture fund investment (contributions include more than just dollars) by real estate companies has also picked up drastically in 2017. Realogy (realogy.com) and independent brokerage network Leading Real Estate Companies of the World (leadingre.com) have both invested in

Real Estate-Focused VCs and Accelerators

In recent years, real estate has seen a handful of real estate-focused venture capital firms and accelerator programs crop up, including two real estate-focused venture funds in just the last 24 months: Moderne Ventures and Fifth Wall. These new venture capital firms add significant real estate funding power to established real estate companies who participate in them.

Founded in 2015, Moderne Ventures (moderneventures.com) directs its $33 million fund toward early-stage companies with products and services applicable to the real estate, finance, insurance and home services industries. Strategic investors include Realogy and Leading Real Estate Companies of the World. Some of Moderne Ventures' investments include Better Mortgage (better.com), Mortgage Hippo (mortgagehippo.com), Contactually (contactually.com) and TaskEasy (taskeasy.com). The firm also operates Moderne Passport, an immersion program focused on customer acquisition and growth.

Launched in 2016, Fifth Wall is a VC "focused on technology solutions for the Built World" – in other words, real estate -- with $240 million to invest. It defines the Built World as "the canvas of human existence, it is where we live, where we work, where we sleep, where we consume, where we move, where we create, where we connect, and where we play." Its founders include Brad Greiwe, co-founder of Invitation Homes, the nation's largest single-family home rental landlord.

Fifth Wall built its fund with investment from a set of anchor partners dominant in various real estate categories such as Lennar (lennar.com) in homebuilding, CBRE (cbre.com) in commercial real estate brokerage, Lowe's (lowes.com) in home improvement and Equity Residential (equityapartments.com) in multifamily real estate investment. The anchors deliver strategic support to startups by providing distribution, testing, industry expertise, deep insight into processes, pain points and more.

In the residential category, Fifth Wall is most interested in home liquidity and transaction technology, construction technology and mortgage tech, according to Vik Chawla, a senior associate with the fund focused on its residential opportunity. Fifth Wall has invested $65 million of its $240 million fund through November 2017. Opendoor is one of its notable investments in the real estate space. It participated in the Direct Buyer's December 2016 round.

> "A new group of 'outsiders' and investors have turned their eyes toward real estate."

Moderne Ventures (moderneventures.com), a venture fund launched in 2015 that focuses on early-stage real estate startups. Major real estate leaders Hines, CBRE, Equity Residential, Lennar and Rudin Management are strategic investors in real estate-focused VC Fifth Wall. Both Fifth Wall and Moderne Ventures work with their strategic investors to provide their portfolio companies assistance and advice to grow and test the market. Cushman & Wakefield (cushmanwakefield.com) recently partnered with the real estate-focused accelerator MetaProp to provide MetaProp fund and accelerator participants access to the large distributed company as a testing ground and potential client.

Leading residential real estate technology companies continue to be active technology investors and acquirers. Zillow and Move Inc. acquired 10 and

Other real estate-focused VCs and accelerators include (in reverse chronological order of founding):

- MetaProp (metaprop.org): Founded in 2015, MetaProp invests in pre-seed and seed-stage technology and data-driven software and hardware startups within all real estate categories. The firm also operates an accelerator program. Notable investments by MetaProp include Betterview (betterview.net) and Rentalutions (rentalutions.com).

- Traverse Venture Partners (traversevp.com): Founded in 2015, Traverse acts as both an investor and deployment partner for companies aiming to improve the economic or environmental performance of buildings and the real estate industry.

- Brick & Mortar Ventures (brickmortar.vc): Founded in 2014, Brick & Mortar invests in software and hardware solutions for the architecture, engineering, construction and facilities management industries.

- Elmspring (elmspringaccelerator.com) – Launched in 2014, Elmspring's seed-stage accelerator focuses on real estate tech startups.

- Second Century Ventures (SCV, secondcenturyventures.com): The National Association of Realtors initially capitalized SCV in 2008. SCV primarily focuses investment on software-as-a-service companies focused on big data applications, digital media, financial tech and business services that address real estate but can span into other verticals. SCV also operates a growth accelerator, REach, for earlier stage companies. The SCV portfolio includes SmartZip, Updater (updater.com) and DocuSign (docusign.com). Note that the T3 Sixty U.S. real estate technology landscape analysis excludes DocuSign because it is used widely in a variety of industries.

- Camber Creek (cambercreek.com): Founded in 2009, Camber Creek offers strategic support and capital to technology companies focused on the real estate market. The firm's investments include VTS, 42 Floors (42floors.com), Fundrise (fundrise.com) and TaskEasy (taskeasy.com).

- Navitas (navitascap.com): Also founded in 2009, Navitas focuses on investing at the intersection of the energy and information technology categories in real estate, with specific domain expertise on intelligent buildings and enterprise startups. Notable Navitas investments include Truss and Matterport.

seven technology companies, respectively, between 2010 and 2015, a period when both firms significantly upped their acquisition activity. In the last two years, Zillow Group acquired Naked Apartments (nakedapartment.com) and Bridge Interactive (bridgeinteractive.com), Hampton Real Estate Online (hreo.com) and New Home Feed. In 2017, Zillow Group also led a financing round for augmented reality technology company Hutch. Move Inc. and parent company News Corp. have also recently made investments in Matterport and acquired home and garden design sites Remodelista (remodelista.com) and Gardenista (gardenista.com).

Fidelity National Financial Inc. (fnf.com) has also added to its real estate tech portfolio through recent investments: a 2016 acquisition of Commissions, Inc. (commissionsinc.com), a 2017 acquisition of RealGeeks CRM (realgeeks.com) and a majority stake in digital transaction management platform SkySlope (skyslope.com) in 2017.

Takeaway

Two decades ago, a group made up predominantly of "outsiders" burst onto the residential real estate brokerage scene and attempted to restructure the industry. Their attempts largely centered on two strategies – a consolidation play and technology innovation play. HFS acquired Century 21, ERA Real Estate, Coldwell Banker and PHH Mortgage, and Berkshire Hathaway acquired HomeServices of America. On the technology side, Bank of America announced huge plans to automate the homebuying transaction, NAR helped create and launch realtor.com and a slew of dot-com companies such as HomeBid, HomeGain and HomeAdvisor secured funding and launched.

An estimated $4 billion was invested at that time and although many initiatives did not survive the dot-com bubble, that investment led to the creation of the two largest real estate companies the industry has ever seen – Realogy and HomeServices of America.

Twenty years later the real estate industry is more consolidated – both Realogy and HSA have acquired a large number of companies (see Chapter No. 5, "Brokerage M&A Momentum Broadens.") – and the industry is significantly more technologically advanced thanks to powerful, newer players such as Zillow Group, DocuSign, CoreLogic (corelogic.com), Black Knight Financial Services (bkfs.com) and many more. Realogy Holdings invested heavily in technology with its 2014 acquisition of tech-focused brokerage ZipRealty for $166 million. The firm adapted ZipRealty into its in-house tech innovation hub, ZapLabs (zaplabs.com).

> "New brands (such as Redfin, Compass and Opendoor) have become billion dollar enterprises almost overnight."

The U.S. real estate industry however still has immense room for technology innovation, and investors have taken notice. In 2017, a new group of "outsiders" and investors have turned their eyes toward real estate. Although funding is still spread across both smaller early-stage companies as well as large, later-stage firms, the year-over-year increase in investments in our industry and 2017's sky-high funding indicates that we may be near a tipping point. New brands (such as Redfin, Compass and Opendoor) are becoming billion dollar enterprises almost overnight while many old-guard traditional brokerage companies are watching the relevance of their business models and the value of their brands decline.

The industry must pay attention to the new business models, the latest technology and each well-funded new innovation. The years between 2015 and 2020, just like the period between 1995 and 2000, may determine the dominant companies for decades to come.

Annual Leadership Think Tank

T3 Summit

The invite-only event for CEOs and C-level executives in real estate.

2018 T3 Summit
April 10-12, 2018
Miami, Florida

t3summit.com
t360.com

2017/2016 Residential Category Funding

Company	2017 Funding through Dec. 7 (in millions)	Funding Type
Compass	$550.0	Series E, F
Houzz	$400.0	Series E
OfferPad	$260.0	Debt/Equity
HouseCanary	$64.0	Series B
Placester	$50.0	Series D
HomeLight	$40.0	Series B
Updater	$45.0	Institutional Placement
Knock	$32.5	Series A
Opcity	$27.0	Series A
Amitree	$14.1	Series A
Hutch	$10.0	Series A
Pro.com	$10.0	Equity
Reali	$8.0	Series A
Whichdoor	$8.0	Series A
Matterport	$5.0	Equity
Centriq Technology Inc	$4.8	Equity
Agentology	$4.5	Series A
Homebot	$4.5	Seed
TripleMint	$4.5	Series A
Trelora	$4.4	Equity
AdWerx	$4.3	Series A
Home61	$4.0	Seed
RealConnex	$3.5	Equity
Riley	$3.1	Seed
Property Simple	$3.0	Equity
Door Inc	$2.8	Series A
Bedly	$2.7	Seed
Gridics	$2.7	Seed
Flip	$2.2	Seed
Houwzer	$2.0	Seed
Rentalutions	$2.0	Seed
GoldenKey	$1.8	Equity
Sweepbright	$1.6	Series A
First.io	$1.6	Seed
Faira	$1.5	Seed
HouseLens	$1.0	Series B
RealScout	$0.9	Debt
Remine	$0.8	Seed
Walkthrough	$0.4	Angel
Imprev	$0.2	Equity
Virtual Xperience Inc.	$0.2	Seed

Company	2016 funding (in millions)	Funding Type
Opendoor	$210.0	Series D
Compass	$75.0	Series C
Apartment List	$30.0	Series B
Updater	$23.0	Equity
Zumper	$17.6	Series B
Rooomy	$13.0	Series B
SmartZip	$12.0	Debt
HomeLight	$11.0	Series A
Real	$9.5	Equity
Cozy	$8.5	Series B
Homie	$8.3	Seed
Hutch	$5.0	Series A
Onerent	$5.0	Seed/Series A
RealScout	$4.4	Series A
Contactually	$3.0	Debt
Property Simple	$3.0	Equity
Real Savvy	$2.7	Series A
Castle	$2.5	Seed
Baroo	$2.3	Seed
Knock	$2.0	Seed
Reali	$2.0	Seed
Relola	$1.7	Seed
GoldenKey	$1.1	Equity
ReaLync	$1.1	Seed
Home61	$1.0	Seed
VeryApt	$1.0	Seed
Househappy	$0.9	Equity
HomeSpotter	$0.9	Debt
Door Inc.	$0.8	Seed
BombBomb	$0.7	Debt
Imprev	$0.6	Debt
Spacio	$0.4	Seed
Realvolve	$0.3	Debt
FrontDoor	$0.3	Debt
CurbCall	$0.2	Seed

2017/2016 Mortgage Category Funding

Company	2017 Funding through Dec. 1 (in millions)	Funding Type
Blend	$100.00	Series D
LendingHome	$56.60	Series C
Better Mortgage	$15.00	Series B
Cloudvirga	$15.00	Series B
Lenda	$5.30	Series A
Morty	$3.00	Seed
MortgageHippo	$2.30	Seed
Approved	$1.00	Seed
	2016 funding (in millions)	
Blend	$40.00	Series C
Better Mortgage	$30.00	Series A
Clara Lending	$24.30	Debt/Series A
LoanLogics	$10.00	Series B
Point	$8.40	Series A
Cloudvirga	$7.50	Series A
Maxwell	$1.40	Angel/Seed
Morty	$0.30	Angel
Lendsnap	$0.10	Seed

2017/2016 Commercial Category Funding

Company	2017 Funding through Dec. 7 (in millions)	Funding Type
Cadre	65	Series C
RealtyShares	$39.90	Series C
Roofstock	$35.00	Series C
TaskEasy	$21.30	Series C
Fundrise	$14.50	Equity
CrediFi	$13.00	Series B
Honest Buildings	$13.00	Series B
Truss	$9.00	Series A
BuildOut	$8.00	Series A
Apto	$7.50	Equity
BetterView	$2.00	Equity
Enertiv	$1.50	Equity
	2016 funding (in millions)	
SMS Assist	$150.00	Series D
Buildium	$65.00	Equity
VTS	$55.00	Series C
RealtyShares	$53.80	Series B/Debt/Equity
Cadre	$50.00	Series B
HomeUnion	$16.00	Series B
TaskEasy	$12.00	Series B
Rentlytics	$9.20	Series A
HappyCo	$7.50	Series A
Compstak	$4.50	Equity
CREXi	$4.30	Seed
CrowdStreet	$3.50	Series A
Click Notices	$2.00	Equity
BetterView	$1.60	Seed
Realty Mogul	$1.50	Equity
IdealSpot	$1.30	Seed
redIQ (Resimodel)	$1.00	Debt/Seed
Honest Buildings	$1.00	Debt

Stefan Swanepoel, CEO
stefan@t360.com
(949) 202-5758

Jack Miller, President
jack@t360.com
(512) 772-4341

Tinus Swanepoel, EVP
tinus@t360.com
(949) 397-2107

(949) 627-8877
t360.com

About T3 Sixty

Since 1997 we have identified and analyzed hundreds of trends, business models and shifts that have impacted the residential real estate industry. Many were accurately detailed years before they became part of the mainstream.

Our suite of regular reports and studies include:

- Swanepoel Trends Report (annually since 2006)
- Technology Guides (biannually since 2010)
- Swanepoel Power 200 (annually since 2014)

We have also published dozens of white papers and case studies since 1999, including major national studies such as:

- The Definitive Analysis of Negative Game Changes Emerging in Real Estate (DANGER Report)
- The Canadian DANGER Report
- The Commercial Real Estate Analysis of the Latest Emerging Risks and Trends (CRE ALERT)
- The MLS 2020 Agenda

T3 Sixty doesn't create the news. We don't report the news. We analyze the news and understand why it happens and what impact it may have. We help reduce the noise in the real estate industry so you can make better decisions.

Understanding innovation, change and new business models in real estate, especially before the rest of your competition does, enables you to create strategies that give you an advantage. Countless companies have ignored change and suffered the consequences. Don't be one of them.

Although no one can exactly predict the future, you can find double-digit growth if you know where to look. Constant exploration and systematic analysis provide insights that can be as valuable as market intelligence, if not more so.

And that is what T3 Sixty provides business leaders: a multidisciplined and experienced consulting team focused on finding the answers and on solving problems.

If you would like to explore how you can leverage T3 Sixty to your benefit, let's have a confidential conversation to explore your options.